THE *Fight* FOR *Family*

Defeating Generational Dysfunction,
Finding Generational Freedom

Francie Willis

With

Brooke Willis, Grayson Leak, Keaton Leak,
Alli Willis, Brittany Willis, Ciera Willis
and
Joan L. Turley and Dr. Mark Williams

The Fight For Family: Defeating Generational
Dysfunction, Finding Generational Freedom

@2019 Francie Willis

In Association with:

Elite Online Publishing
63 East 11400 South Suite #230
Sandy, UT 84070
https://EliteOnlinePublishing.com

ISBN: 978-1708495053

Endorsements

"The Fight for Family," comes at a time when many families are searching for help with their own family dysfunction. Now more than ever before, we live in a world that continues to be filled with anxiety and stress. Divorce, alcoholism, addictions, and abandonment have continued to plague families for generations. Willis writes from her learned experiences and wisdom of five generations of family challenges.

This book offers practical ideas, and Biblical truths that may produce a lifetime of healing. Viewpoints concerning the challenges young adults face today with family dysfunction are discussed by the author's grandchildren and co-writers, in a fresh new perspective."

-Dr. Victor L.M. Graves
Retired Pastor, and Corresponding Writer for Early Christian Writings, and the Baptist Press News, Formed in 1946 by the Southern Baptist Convention.

"Francie Willis's grandchildren have all overcome dysfunction in their family lives. Today all eight of these young adults have either graduated from college or are attending major universities. I have known Francie Willis for over 30 years, and I believe this book will help other families who have dysfunction in various forms, to recognize and fight dysfunction in order to live a successful healthy life."

-Sue Burnett,
President, Burnett Specialists.
2019 Texas Business Woman of the Year.

"Francie Willis has written a must-read book for anyone considering confronting dysfunction in the family. Issues are discussed that have occurred from generations of neglect and selfishness that continue to erode family health and happiness. I believe this could be anyone's family today. Tapping into God's word, to bring complete understanding and clarity about the issues, provides another insight into the subject matter. It takes honesty, determination and courage to write about family dysfunction, it was refreshing to read the grandchildren's thoughts and perspectives."

-Janice Hall
Teacher, The Church of St. John the Devine, Houston, Texas

"In the Gospel of John, Jesus informs us that in this world we will have trouble. Trouble from the enemy, trouble from the world and trouble from our own flesh. Unfortunately, our sinful and destructive behavior can painfully echo down our family corridors for generations. Francie Willis, in The Fight For Family, reminds us that that the second half of John 16:33 is just as true as the first part- that we can take heart, because Christ has overcome the world! This is especially true in overcoming and healing the generational brokenness that all families have encountered since sin entered the world. Just ask Adam and Eve.

Francie reminds us that sin doesn't get the final word. With the loving insight of a mother and grandmother, Francie applies biblical wisdom and the hope of the Gospel to help break the cycle of generational dysfunction. And as she shares lessons and helpful tools from her personal journey, we are reminded that we can indeed take heart in Christ's victory. Thanks, Francie, for leading the way toward freedom and taking the risk to call the first Santa Fe Summit."

-John Garrett Jr.

"I was so surprised and excited to learn that my dear friend of almost 40 years, Francie Willis, has undertaken to help families curb the issue that plagues many of us...dysfunctional maladies within the family unit.

"Francie is the right person at the right time to approach this tragedy from a Biblical and generational viewpoint. When I read the book I discovered her insight into how to manage, grow and thrive in spite of the conflicts so many of us are familiar with and seek answers for healing.

"I trust Francie's Biblical knowledge as a committed Christian, as well as her amazing experiences over the years raising 5 *children/stepchildren and being a devoted wife, business woman and the most beautiful friend anyone could ask for."*

-Diane Ray
Interior Designer, 30 year Adult Bible Teacher.
Wife and Mother

Dedication

For my great nephew Drake,
you are the spark God used
to ignite our passion for this book

With love . . .
to my great niece Sophia,
to my great nephews
Alex, Santiago, William, and Finn,
and to my grandchildren:
Brooke, Keaton, Allison, Grayson,
Brittany, Ciera, Trevor, & Jake

GITTINGS

TABLE OF CONTENTS

Foreword

The first time I met Francie Willis, she was behind glass doors to the executive office of Urban Retreat, a Texas luxury day spa she led to success with recognition from leading industry magazines and many more accolades from numerous sources. Knowing of her stellar reputation, I trembled a little as I walked towards her office until I was in her presence." Is that fear I see in your face?" she asked. Then she said, "We will have none of that." Our initial meeting lasted two hours. It was during that time that I saw the incredible heart of Francie Willis for the community and those around her. I loved her immediately when I discerned the depth of her faith and her stubborn insistence that love never fails.

After almost twenty years of friendship, it was my utmost pleasure to read her book and to see in writing what I saw lived out in her life. I was thrilled to see her experiences recorded in writing, to be passed down to our current generation and for generations to come. Although she referred to herself as a seventy-year-old grandmother, she is more than the grandmother who baked pies or made Christmas special for the family. Against the backdrop of family dysfunction, the complexity of blended families and a history of alcohol consumption among family members, she dared to fight for the "uncommon story" and invited her grandchildren on the journey with her. She insisted the "common story" is what the world expects from dysfunction but hers will be the 'uncommon story' when family members come together to communicate in honesty and make decisions on what they want their future to be like, as compared to just letting life happen to them.

Written with the warmth of a grandmother, with the faith of a believer, with the boldness of a fighter, with the passion of a woman who dared to say, "enough is enough", this book will offer you hope and courage to leave a broken past and shape the future.

-Anita Carmen, Founder and President
Inspire Women

Acknowledgements

I offer my deepest gratitude to the following people
for their part in my life and my book:

Joan L. Turley and Dr. Mark Williams: *my writing and editing team*

Michael Willis: *my husband.*

John & Mary Lambert Willis: *my in-laws.*

Stacey Ann and James P. Baker: *my maternal grandparents.*

Rose and Pangrazio Marchione: *my paternal grandparents.*

Anita and Frank Marchione: *my parents.*

Gary Marchione: *my brother.*

Abbie and Jerry Tyner, Charles Tyner: *my daughter's grandparents and father.*

Tamara Leak: *my daughter and mother of my grandsons.*

Kyle Leak: *father of my grandsons.*

Mike Willis Jr: *my son and father of my granddaughters and grandson.*

Lyndalin Willis: *mother of my granddaughters and grandson.*

Mark Willis: *my son and father of my granddaughters and grandson.*

Dawn Willis: *mother of my granddaughters and grandson.*

Deborah Willis Tatham: *our daughter.*

Anita Carmen: *my friend and founder of Inspire Women.*

Molly Maledon Arp: *godmother of my daughter and my friend for 61 years.*

June Nance: *my friend.*

Generations of My Family: *Past, Present, and Future.*

Introduction
A MOMENT IN TIME

It was just a cell phone photo: nothing fancy, just a moment in time, captured through the lens of a camera. The unsuspecting subject of the portrait was a grandfather cradling a newborn baby boy. But it was that look of immeasurable joy and immense wonder on the grandfather's face that drew me in, took my breath away, stole my heart, and captured all my love because that doting grandfather was my *only* brother and the child held in his arms was his *only* grandson.

Well, I knew in an instant that I would love that baby forever ... just like I loved my brother.

Talk about joy—this was a moment to celebrate! I pinched the photo to zoom-in for a closer look. I did not want to miss a single thing. I wanted to take in every detail of my brother's once-in-a-lifetime moment—holding that beautiful baby boy for the very first time. I studied that photo like it was a priceless work of art!

I could see the fine crinkled laugh lines etched around my brother's eyes that sparkled with undeniable pride and joy. I gazed adoringly at that precious baby's face and then I glanced back at my brother's face and was immediately struck by how much this tiny new baby looked like his grandfather. He was the spitting image of Gary! And gosh, isn't that every grandfather's dream—to see his likeness passed down from generation to generation?

Well, Gary certainly had a look-alike in this little boy! There could be no denying the new baby boy was a Marchione if ever there was one. And honest to goodness, I am not sure what happened, but looking at that photo of the little boy who looked just like my brother—stirred up a flood of memories. I took a thoughtful walk down memory lane. The results were beautiful, in part, because even though I was "the oldest child" and "my brother's big sister", I was never the one to do the "looking after" and the "taking care of." Nope. The roles were always reversed. From the time Gary was old enough to understand that I was his big sister, he became my protector and caretaker. A girl could not have asked for a better brother than Gary. He was my hero and the memories were sweet!

TIME CHANGES PERSPECTIVE

As the oldest child I had "all the breaks". I had every advantage in the world, including a fully funded junior college education. By the time my brother graduated from high school, my parents were unable to pay full tuition for his college education. Times were hard. Gary had to go to work while taking night classes at a small junior college. Subsequently, he never had the opportunity to experience some of the joys and privileges and opportunities that were given to me. He never traveled the world, never experienced cultures beyond our borders (other than Belize and Mexico), never wanted to move in the elite circles of the movers and the shakers. But what a great brother he was!

Yes, in a way, that picture wrecked me. It stirred up a fierce love for a little boy that I had yet to hold just because he looked so much like my brother—the man who had grown up to become my hero. Through every season of life, even on his worst days, Gary never stopped wanting the very best for me, never stopped being proud of me and was always genuinely happy for every good thing that ever came my way. I could not have asked for a better brother.

IT ONLY TAKES A MOMENT

Yes, this was surely a "nothing can steal my joy" kind of moment.

But ironically, without warning, my emotions shifted. Out of the blue, in the middle of this abundant dose of happiness, I was overwhelmed with a profound sense of sorrow that almost knocked me to the ground.

This was an uninvited and unwelcome emotion that showed up out of nowhere, attempting to take root in my soul. Trying to understand what had just happened, I looked back at the photo and thought "How in the world had I gone from total joy to profound sadness in the blink of an eye?"

Suddenly I saw it. I knew the cause of the ache in my soul and the break in my heart. There it was in the photo—two precious blood-bound lives: one so full of hope and fresh potential with a beautiful unblemished future, the other marred by broken dreams and disappointments drowned in and diluted by alcohol. It made me sad. I wanted to cry right then and there.

Words began to form in my mind. And before I could reel them in or take them back, I spoke those words into existence: "I do not want to see this beautiful baby boy follow in his family's footsteps which have been muddied in way too many years of drinking. I want something more for this child!" Please do not get me wrong! I love my brother and my family! But I am old enough to know that too many beers and alcohol robbed many family members of some great moments in their lifetime's.

So, yes, in that moment of sadness I said it! It felt like a prophetic word and I was not about to take it back. But it shook me to my core as my thoughts continued, "What in the world can we do to help this little boy not become an alcoholic? How can we ensure a better future for him?"

In that moment, I was determined that things needed to change for generations to come. Not only did I want change for this new little life that I had fallen madly in love with before I ever held him, I wanted change for every single grandchild, niece, and nephews who affectionately call me "Mia". Things had to change! We had to give them a way to embrace and to live a better future.

MOMENTS TURN INTO YEARS

I felt the weight of what had been awakened within me and entrusted to my care. I knew there would be no turning back. It was time to draw a line in the sand and say, "Enough is enough". And then, as if to underscore the seriousness of that moment, the words of the old Grammy-winning Harry Chapin song "Cat's in the Cradle" began to play over and over in my mind. I do not believe for one moment that this song surfaced in my mind coincidentally. Nothing underscores the fact that one generation impacts the next generation like that song.

Just look at the opening lyrics ...

"My child arrived just the other day
He came into the world in the usual way
But there were planes to catch and bills to pay
He learned to walk while I was away
And he was talking 'fore I knew it, and as he grew
He'd say, "I'm gonna be like you, dad
You know I'm gonna be like you."

The song kept playing in my mind until the insightful powerful phrase in the last verse of this same song "He'd grown up just like me, my boy was just like me" drove home the urgency of the matter at hand. Like it or not, every preceding generation impacts the generations that follow—be it negative or positive, be it intentional or unintentional. We are responsible for the impact we make upon the next generation. I could not help but think of my precious brother having struggled with the burden of his business losses, the brokenness of his relationships, and the damaging impact of his drinking. And then, as fast as I was overwhelmed with sadness and sorrow, my resolve rapidly grew even stronger—so much so, that I knew I had to do something.

A LOOK AT THE PAST

But I did not know *what* to do. I did not have a plan. I did not have a clue. All I knew was *I needed to do something* that could change the results of the next generation becoming like us—we have been so busted and broken. If change was going to happen, it must start with me—I needed to find the way to help my family live the better life God has intended for them, the life He created them to live—a meaningful flourishing abundant life, full of hope and great joy!

If ever there was a hope to be found, I sensed we needed to stop pretending there was nothing wrong or that nothing could be done. There is truth to be told—everything is not alright and has not been for generations in our family—from those who have gone before us to those of us who are still alive. We have all made mindless mistakes, suffered, and abused. We have all blown it one way or another. It's the story of humanity. No one gets through life without a few scars and some deep hurts along the way.

This is the unfolding of our story of brokenness and the hope that can be found in the telling of our tales, around a table of love, in the Presence of The One Who can make all things new. Can you relate? Maybe this is your family too?

With the cell phone photo still cradled in the palm of my hands, I made an unbreakable commitment to start telling the truth. Being totally honest with you—I know that could mean costly risk. But I know this: the risk of doing nothing ... the risk of not taking action ... will be more expensive to me and others, than the risk I am unwilling to take. If anything is real to me about this, here is one example of many: this cannot and will not be an experience of "The Blame Game." No one is to be blamed, but everyone is responsible for their own future. It is a choice to respond and not react to the past that will create the future God wants *for us* and we want *more and more* for ourselves. I could waste my time blaming myself, but my time is more precious with every passing day. Each day must count—this I know.

If healing is to come, it must start with someone and that someone is me. I need to be willing to look at the past—not to focus or fixate on the past in the sense of "fixing it," because we cannot do that, no one can. But we can shine a light on the past, acknowledge the pain of broken promises and deep hurts and honestly admit: "Well, this happened, then that happened, and that is how we got from there to here." And in doing that, we are no longer pretending—we are telling the truth and we are creating safe places to work through our pain and into our potential.

So, as the beautiful faces of every grandchild, niece, and nephew flashed before my eyes, a simple plan began to formulate. I made a mental agreement not to brush things under the rug of the past and not to ignore the elephant in the room that we had all gotten rather good at ignoring—as if ignoring could wipe away the awful behaviors that we have done to one another and that have been done to us. These behaviors have impacted all our lives.

In being willing to sit in that moment with the weight of the sorrow of those shifting emotions from ecstatic joy to profound sadness—while allowing painful memories to surface for the purpose of securing a better future for my grandchildren, niece, and nephews, it was as if the film of my life passed before my eyes frame by frame.

Only this time, I was seeing those memories with new eyes—I was sensing a rising fresh hope that would become a way to move the grandkids forward over the speed bumps of life. If not talked about in an open non-judgmental setting, the memories could become obstacles to the bright future that God has planned for them all.

THERE HAS TO BE MORE

What we think "we know for sure" always seems to be far greater than "everything we do not yet know." We are tempted to hold on to "what we know," because it is all we know. But, in truth, "what we do not yet know" is really far greater, because God is far greater than all we can ask, think, or imagine."[1] So ... there has to be more to this life we have experienced so far, there has to be more that God has in store for us.

We are not His greatest challenge. He is not worried about us—because He knows we cannot fail when we trust and depend on Him to work transformation through our cooperation with Him. We are not *impossible* for Him.

I understand that "some of the people I know and love" will take a closer look at my life and quickly find the messes that have been made and the hearts that have been broken because of unwise needless choices and say:

> "How could it be that anything good could come out of all these mindless things, these insensitive hurts, these destructive habits?
> How in the world do you hope for a better future for your children's children?"

Honestly, in my humanity, I might be tempted to say the same thing. I for sure would be tempted to say the same thing, if I decided to listen to all the negative talk and the self-limiting beliefs that others so freely embrace. If I listened to them, I would be tempted to believe that my life and the lives of those I love are utterly hopeless.

Oh, believe me, I have heard it all. If I have heard it once, I have heard it a thousand times:

> "Francie, just get used to it. It is what it is. Accept things for what they are."

Never—because if I did that, it really would be hopeless! I might as well just roll over and die because I do not believe for a minute that the future of the next generation is hopeless. For that matter, I do not believe that our generation is hopeless either. Whatever is required of me and however God wants to use me to ensure hope, I commit myself to that!

I have been told more times than I care to admit:

"For goodness sake Francie, open up your eyes. You cannot
fix anything.
We know you have tried to be good all your life,
but your God is just a crutch and nothing more."

Many times, "what is good and true about you" will be twisted by the enemy through the "I am only trying to spare you the agonizing disappointment" words of people who claim they simply want to help you. The enemy's goal is to cut us deeply, immobilize us, and delay or destroy our destiny. Their words only define, delay, or destroy you, if you allow them to take root in you.

What I know is this: I am a child of God, a daughter of my Father, the King of all creation, a disciple of Jesus, and someone who knows that nothing is impossible for Him!

GOD IS NOT A CRUTCH

When I hear those little digs, the Presence of Someone infinitely powerful rises up in me and I know that I know that I know ... I am not hopeless! My family is not hopeless! God is not my crutch! He is so much more than a crutch! He is unlimited Power! He is the Redeemer of all things! He is The One Who makes all things new!

When I look at everything that has gone on in the past and everything that is going on in the present ... in the natural things would appear to be hopeless. So far, I have not been able to do anything about it. So far, my family has not either. But the God who has held me together all these years still can transform my family.

So, I began to pray: "God, show us what to do about all this. There is more to life than this and enough is enough!"

But, let me be perfectly clear: It is not just me saying "Enough is enough!" It is not just my family saying, "Enough is enough!"

The God of all creation is saying to us and through us "Enough is enough!" because He did not come into our lives to just stick crutches under our arms so we could hobble along in life. *He came to "make all things new!"*[2]

Are you already saying: "Oh my gosh—I can so relate to this story? This is my family too!" If so, keep reading!

May you find the courage to start telling the truth with the people you love—those that matter the most in the world to you.

Chapter One
The Heart of The Santa Fe Summit

We never know when a moment in time will completely change the trajectory of our lives. We awaken to a fresh new day while thinking it is life as usual. A cup of coffee and a kiss on the cheek and we are out the door to live life to its fullest. Carpe Diem! But we "do not know when" that something is coming that will impact our lives and we will never be the same again. When it comes, we are never able to go back to life as usual. In just a mere moment in time, everything has changed.

These life-altering moments happen to everyone. We cannot escape them. Life just happens. We meet the love of our life, or we discover there has been an affair. We lose a job and we're offered a job, but it's halfway around the world. We think we are just going to hear a speaker, but the message wrecks the comfort zone of our soul and changes our perspective. We can never go back to life as usual ... because ... we cannot un-hear the words both spoken and heard.

These kinds of things catch us off guard. Though we are unprepared, a response is required of us. We can either do nothing (which is a decision in itself) or we can rise to the challenge to become the best version of ourselves that we ever dreamed possible. The choice is always ours to make.

THE PHOTO THAT FANNED THE FLAME

On the day the photo popped up on my cell phone screen, I was not expecting that beautiful photo of a precious newborn baby boy would change the trajectory of my life. But it did. All it took was one glance and, in the blink of an eye, a spark ignited in my soul. I had a choice. I could put a lid on that spark to make it nothing more than a dying ember or I could invite the Holy Spirit to blow upon the spark to transform the beginnings of a flame into a burning fire that would change the destiny of my family. I responded. I chose to ask Him.

You see, even thinking about all the experiences of disappointment and disillusionment that had come into my sweet brother's life just about broke my heart all over again. I am convinced some of those disappointments were at the root of his battle with alcoholism. Like most men his age, disappointments with work and relationships falling apart tears at the core of your confidence and prompts you to do most anything to make the pain go away.

My brother Gary was a good man and a good father. He adored his son Ty who practically worshipped the ground his father walked on. My brother's little boy loved his father something fierce like many little boys do. But his dad drank too much. It was hard on everyone because everyone loved my brother—especially his little boy.

Imagine that, when that little guy was just ten years old, he was overjoyed to find out that his dad was going to a rehab facility to "get better." That eight-week period went by somewhat quickly for all of us—but, for that little boy who spent every day anticipating the day his dad would come home, it felt like eternity. Time seemed to move about as fast as molasses in January.

At last, the day had come when my brother was to be released from rehab to reunite with his family once again. Everyone was ecstatic with anticipation of what the future would hold after rehab. It was a "promised fresh start" for everyone. On the day Gary was to arrive home, his wife (who was stepmom to Ty) made sure the house was clean and tidy, sparkling on the inside as well as the outside. This was going to be a great day and a new beginning.

While putting the final touches on their home, she noticed some leaves had landed on the eaves of the house. She wanted a picture-perfect homecoming for her husband and those leaves distracted from the well-manicured lawn and landscaping. Making a last-minute decision to remove the visible clutter, she climbed up a ladder to blow off the leaves from the roof line.

However, in the process of the climb, my sister-in-law lost her balance, fell from the ladder, and suffered compound fractures to both ankles. She laid on the ground with bones protruding through her skin for two excruciating hours until a neighbor found her and called an ambulance. In unbearable pain, she was immediately transported to the nearest hospital and quickly sedated by medical personnel.

In the meantime, my brother arrived at the airport. He could hardly wait to embrace his wife and see his son again. He had missed them so much, but neither of them was waiting for him there.

He waited, and waited, and he waited. Still, no one came. Two hours later and deeply disappointed, he hailed a cab only to arrive to an empty home. Much to his dismay, his wife was not there either to greet him —there was no joyous homecoming celebration whatsoever. There was nothing—nothing but an empty house.

It was not until a short time later that he heard about his wife's terrible accident and that she was in the hospital with serious injuries. After eight long weeks of intensive rehab, doing hard soul-work which had revived the hope that life could be better for him and his family—this was his "Welcome Home." For the next six months, my sister-in-law could not walk, could not work, went through three surgeries, and lived in constant pain. At best, we could call it "an extremely stressful time". Eventually, under the strain of it all, my brother Gary relapsed. He fell back into the familiar comfort of cracking open a few too many cold beers. When my brother's little boy saw his dad with a beer in his hand, he was brokenhearted. More than anything in the world, he wanted a dad who did not drink. Gary was never a drunk. He worked every day of his life and never turned away from extending a helping hand. He would give the shirt off his back if someone was in need. But he drank too much which impacted the lives of those he loved and ultimately his own life.

As life went on, Gary's boy grew up and spent long weekends on the lake with the dad that he loved who was consistently found kicking back in his favorite chair with an iced cold can of beer in his hand. My brother's son quickly learned to equate "fun and "relaxation" with drinking—they became mentally inseparably bonded. The familiar Harry Chapin song played out before my eyes. I saw it: "I'm gonna be like you, Dad; you know I'm gonna be like you."

Though the drinking was hard to watch in my family, it never stopped me from loving my brother, my nephew, my father, my husband and my son. I wanted to see them free from the alcohol that robbed them of precious moments and deep conversations that could have been shared more often with the children they cherish so much ... if only they had a life free of alcohol.

THE SPARK OF THE SANTA FE SUMMIT

It is most unfortunate that many times as parents we fail to stop to ponder deeply the behaviors we are transferring to our children. A child is like a sponge, waiting to soak up our traits as parents. Our traits immunize them against the standards we spout off or shout out to them. I have said to my own adult children on many occasions: "Just look at your kids. They are video cameras with legs. They follow you around watching your every move. They listen to what you say and mimic you in every way because you are the person they love and trust the most. And yes, they want to be just like you!"

Sadly, many parents do not understand how much of an influence they truly are upon their children. They think it is okay to curse "every time the light turns red when they're in a hurry" or "whenever someone cuts them off in traffic". They think it is okay to drop the "F" bomb every now and then. And then they wonder why their children have issues in school and with other children? They simply do what they see their parents do. I see it everywhere I go, and it is extremely heartbreaking to me.

That is why I knew, when I looked at that photo of my brother Gary, my nephew Ty, and my great nephew Drake (my brother's new grandson), I wanted much more for my entire family. Sadness filled my heart and overtook the joy of that moment. I had to do something!

I had to find a way to show my family and grandchildren there is a better way to deal with our sorrows, our hurts, and our disappointments.

I had to find a way to help them discover that most of our problems are not circumstantial. Most of our problems are perceptual.

I had to show them that "all of our biggest problems can be traced back to our inadequate understanding of who God is"[3] in the middle of our messes. If only we would invite God into our mess so that He could heal those broken places, we would have a way to move forward despite the behaviors that have impacted our lives for generation

It takes a lot for each of us to come to the place where we can sincerely ask ourselves: "What if "*normal to us*" is not "*normal*"? "What if *what we think we know*" is "*not right*"?

It takes a lot for each of us to come to the place where we can admit that we have individually personally been wrong, that none of us is perfect or will be perfect, and that all of us share responsibility for our future. Only then can we put our intention to forgive, heal, and grow into action. Our commitment is to *share reality*, not to *maintain our false perception of reality*. Then "*it happened*" ...

The wheels in my mind began to turn—

What if I could provide a safe place for my grandkids to talk openly and honestly
about their perceptions of the behaviors that had impacted them while growing up?
What if I could provide a place for them?

where there was no shaming, blaming, or condemnation of
anyone?
What would it look like if I could invite them to lay their cards
on the table—
no hiding and no pretending about the things that had
happened in their lives—
things like divorce, abandonment, and addiction that I knew
affected them?
Would that serve to better prepare them for future challenges
they may face
as they enter the adult world?
Could that lead to a better, healthier life for all of them
and for my niece and nephews?
*A plan began to emerge in my mind and real hope began to grow
in my heart—*
I could invite my grandchildren to my home in Santa Fe, New
Mexico.
I could bring them all together
for the sake of acknowledging obstacles and challenges they
might encounter again
in their future if we chose not to talk about their experiences
with them.

I am old enough to know the first step
in setting things right, in reconciliation, in breaking free,
and in healing from broken places
is admitting to ourselves
that something is not right and being willing to say so.
Knowing the truth about our reality comes from
a willingness to talk about our perceptions,

and then being willing to do what is required to forgive, heal, and grow.

So, I could not help but wonder—

What if telling the truth in the company of those we loved most
became the most freeing thing that any of us ever experienced?
What if acknowledging the wrongs that had been done to us
and the wrongs we had done to others
opened the door to forgiveness that we all so desperately need?

This was something I had to do! The stakes were too high to sit back and let a spark of hope become a dying ember.

A plan had been entrusted to my care—there was no turning back—I would host the "Safe Santa Fe Summit" and every grandkid would be invited! There was no turning back. The grandkids were coming to Santa Fe!

BROKENNESS DOES NOT GET THE FINAL WORD

The wheels were set in motion and all I had was a very loose plan to say the least; well ... more like no plan. All I knew was they were all coming alright! My heart was overjoyed because deep inside of me I knew this could be the start of something new, something brave, something that could change the way my grandkids forever looked at their own brokenness.

No one gets through life without brokenness, but God redeems our brokenness and will use everything in our past for good—if we let Him. God has the solution for every problem we have ever faced and will face—but first we must be willing to admit we have problems. There can be no fixing anything, if we will not admit we're in trouble.

Maybe because I have spent most of my life growing up in the shadow of NASA, I understand how critical it is to admit immediately when we have a problem. I mean—what if no one on the NASA space shuttle had been willing to say to the NASA Space Command Center: "Houston, we have a problem"?[4] Well, we would have lost the entire crew of Apollo 13! It was time to say, "We have a problem!" And *I was willing to be the first one to admit it* because I was not about to lose the Willis and Marchione Crew!

GROUND RULES FOR BATTLE

In the weeks leading up to the Safe Santa Fe Summit, I put on my leadership strategy hat and started planning the summit.

Okay, I am going to make a moment for a shameless "grandmother pride" right here:

"I have some very smart grandkids—every single one of them is just brimming over with incredible potential. They are smart as whips. I knew I better have my act together and be ready to bring on my A Game ... because they would certainly be bringing theirs.

"What is it about grandkids, great nieces and nephews" that makes you want to do everything in your power to pave the way for them to be successful? I do not know about you, but they call out the best from me.

Let me now get back on point...

As I began to plan the summit session—this idea of creating a "Battle Board" started stirring in my imagination.

Hmmm ... Battle Board. Rules of Engagement. Strategies to Win the War ...

I started to visualize what needed to happen for our safe summit to be a life-changing collaboration for all of us. Ground Rules would need to be established—

- We would each need to make a commitment to share our perceptions—to be willing to say what were "facts to us" whether true or not.

- We would not judge one another—because that would sabotage the goal to discover the truth which is required to set us free.

- Each participant would be asked to share perceptions of past behaviors—the one sharing would then identify one specific "Battle Word" which would describe the impact the behavior had upon their life.

- The "Battle Word" would then be transferred to the "Battle Board" where strategies for overcoming potential challenges and obstacles associated with the "Battle Word" would be discussed in an open honest non-judgmental no shame/no blame forum.

- All participants would commit to listen intently to one another. That way, each participant would both speak and be heard (i.e. this was designed to create an experience for each grandchild where they could share without fear and be heard in love).

In my heart, I knew...this was going to be

THE START OF SOMETHING TRULY GREAT!

And, I could not help but bow my head and thank God for my precious brother Gary and my great nephew Drake because without them this book would never have come into being or to fruition. They are truly the heroes of this unfolding story.

It is my deepest desire that my grandkids, niece and nephews, and every future generation be the beneficiaries of the wisdom we have gleaned together as we committed to speak the truth in love.

May it help all of you to determine that you can overcome any obstacle, get beyond any challenge, and know that you do not have to fall into negative behavior patterns simply because your parents or your grandparents did.

Whatever has impacted your life does not have to define your future. There is a way forward—and that is Our Story, the Good News that this book was written to tell you!

Join us on our journey, page after page, as we discover the power of telling the truth in love!

Defeating Generational Dysfunction, Finding Generational Freedom
Three Empowering Principles with Three Equipping Questions to Fight FOR YOUR FAMILY

CHAPTER ONE

Principle One. We were powerless before Christ gave us access to grace.

Scripture: Romans 5:1-2 (NLT) "...since we have been made right in God's sight by faith, we have peace with God because of what Jesus Christ our Lord has done for us. Because of our faith, Christ has brought us into this place of undeserved privilege [grace] where we now stand, and we confidently and joyfully look forward to sharing God's glory."

Explanation: Stuck in the partialness of our perspectives, we individually held only a piece of the reality we experienced together. Each of us must come to believe that God will show US the pieces each of us is missing. Once those pieces are revealed in "no-shame no-blame conversations", we are then able to receive from God the ability to choose to FORGIVE and we can see what Christ has done for us so that we can move forward TOGETHER.

Question 1.

Why is it so challenging to "bring our experiences and hurts into the light" of His grace?

Question 2.

It has been said: "The ground is level at the foot of the Cross." How does our conversation change when we understand that we each need God's grace to be restored to one another?

Question 3.

How does knowing "we all struggle" and "none of us is deserving" effect our desire to encourage one another?

Principle Two. God designed a process to transform our suffering into hope.

Scripture: Romans 5:3-5 (NIV) "Not only so, but we also rejoice in our sufferings, because we know that suffering produces perseverance; perseverance, character; and character, hope. And hope does not disappoint us, because God has poured out his love into our hearts by the Holy Spirit, Whom He has given us."

Explanation: The road from suffering to hope seems impossible unless we know that it is not driven by our ability to figure it out and make it happen ourselves. Who knows how to make suffering into perseverance? Perseverance into character? Character into hope? God does and He is The One Who drives the process to which we surrender. Our part is to give Him every opportunity to move us forward in the process—HOPE is our DESTINATION.

Question 1.

God does not want you to experience SHAME. How does that TRUTH influence your thinking?

Question 2.

Understanding that suffering produces perseverance, character, then hope...how can this help us move more quickly to hope?

Question 3.

God proved His Love for us when He sent His Holy Spirit to live IN us. How does it feel to know you can depend on His Power rather than depend on your willpower?

Principle Three. We must choose to love each other perfectly by His power.

Scripture: Romans 5:6-8 (NIV) "You see, at just the right time, when we were still powerless, Christ died for the ungodly. Very rarely will anyone die for a righteous man, though for a good man someone might possibly dare to die. But God demonstrates his own love for us in this: While we were still sinners, Christ died for us."

Explanation: God is not waiting for you to fix yourself before He will love you. He already loves you without your belief, understanding, or consent. Through Jesus' death on the cross, *He proved His love through action* that did not *require* explanation. He showed us how to *act* our way into feeling, instead of *feeling* our way into action. Everything begins to change when we understand that we are designed to relate to each other the same way He relates to us.

Question 1.

We were all God's enemies before Jesus paid sin's price with His blood—that did not stop Him from dying for us. How does that reality change your openness to Him? How does that reality change the way you see others?

Question 2.

What role does the CHOICE to FORGIVE play in creating the FEELING of SAFETY? What does *your* forgiveness create for *others*? What does *their* forgiveness create for *you*?

Question 3.

What does God's demonstration of love for you teach you about Him? What does it teach you about how to release your past and about how to demonstrate your love for others?

Drake Marchione age 8   *Gary Marchione age 8*

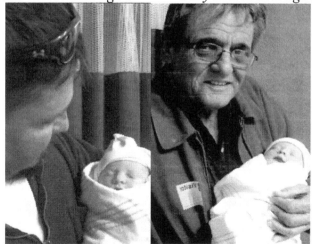

Ty and Drake Marchione
Gary and Drake Marchione 6hrs

Chapter Two
DECIDE TO DO WHATEVER IT TAKES

W hen I hosted the Santa Fe Summit for my grandchildren, I had no way of knowing that it would actually take more than four and half years to write and publish the book you now hold in your hands. However, in hindsight, I can clearly see the hand of God providing. Though each grandchild had clearly identified a "greatest future challenge" that could derail their future success and had thoughtfully devised a strategy for overcoming those potential roadblocks, my grandchildren still needed real-time experience to flesh out their newly formed battle plans.

These last nearly five years have not gone by without challenge or event. The struggles have been real. And yet, how beautiful it has been to watch an overcoming spirit emerge within each grandchild as they have fought for the future that they are learning God has prepared for each one of them, despite their obstacles. They have grown courageous in their efforts.

RESPOND TO THE NUDGE

In taking on this project and delving into all kinds of research, I have discovered that every one of us has been impacted by some form of dysfunction. In her book, Adult Children of Alcoholics,[5] Janet Geringer Woititz has identified and documented thirteen challenges that adults, impacted by addictions and dysfunction in their formative years as children, share in common and consistently encounter (often hidden and seemingly unconscious) at some level during their lifetime. It is amazing to see how prevalent these challenges characteristically show up in our daily lives and explain a lot of our experiences!

What astounds me even more is the fact that God nudged my heart all those years ago (without any knowledge of Janet's book) to create a safe no-shame/no-blame environment for my grandchildren to simply share their perceptions of the issues that had impacted their lives and the challenges they may face in the near future due to those dysfunctions. And what we have discovered is that, in telling the truth in love all those years ago at the Summit, we actually laid a foundation that equipped our hearts to deal head-on with those commonly consistent challenges that all of us seem to face at one time or another. My granddaughter Ciera summed it up beautifully when she said: "If you just keep all the bad things inside of your heart, then you cannot make room to let the good things in." And I think she is on to something big. There's uncommon power available to us when we are willing to bring those challenges out in the open!

DESTRUCTIVE HAND-ME-DOWN DECISIONS

Now, what is especially interesting to me is that some people call these challenges "generational curses"—I call them *destructive hand-me-down decisions.* In them, we often repeat struggle-filled, painful, and destructive choices and patterns passed down from one generation to the next. In a descriptive poetic way, was that not what Harry Chapin was saying every time when we heard him sing "The cat's in the cradle with the silver spoon"? One grandson proudly told me at the start of our journey, "Mia, I understand. But

I will never let the hurtful things that I encountered growing up influence me. I just will not." I must admit that as he said it, I had to wonder, "How can something one sees every single day *not* have a direct and profound impact on their life?"

Granted, my grandson, Keaton, was only eighteen when he made the statement that he would never allow the dysfunction he experienced in his "growing up" years to impact his future choices. You may call me cynical or say I have lived too long in a broken world, yet I questioned how he could be so certain that (somewhere down the road of his personal journey) those hurtful things would not raise their ugly head and subtly creep into his life unaware and trap him. Young minds may question whether dysfunctional choices or actions, from childhood, *should* be the norm, but that is *no guarantee* that these decisions will *not* have a significant influence upon their lives.

As we started this journey, I wanted us to understand the power of both the positive and negative things that impact our lives. So, I did a lot of research, I asked a lot of questions, and I received a myriad of responses regarding *generational curses and blessings.* It is just as clear that there are *powerful-ongoing otherwise-unexplainable factors* that are passed down from one generation to the next—some productive, and some destructive. They most often come in the form of thoughts, understandings, attitudes, choices, words, behaviors, patterns, and habits.

Over the generations, many people have simply laughed off "generational curses" as nonsense. It is "interestingly *funny*" how a *biblical term* can be used, and people will laugh it off. But when a *secular term* is used like "universally *common* challenges", people are more inclined to listen. *Why is that,* when the biblical term has been used for thousands of years, long before Chapin was singing about it or Woititz was writing about it? It is easier to call someone a "loser or lucky".

I also discovered that some people strongly related to specific things they considered were definitely "hand-me-downs" from relatives. Some examples of their responses were among the weirdest things I have ever heard!

Some people told me they did not believe in *generational curses* because "each person has a responsibility to live their own life and make their own way" (I agree). But, my agreement with that line of reasoning does not negate factual proof from well-verified studies that life decisions are based upon influences we share in common. The proof is clearly traced to physiological-psychological-emotional-spiritual impact perspectives which most often have surrounded us throughout our lives and have been consistently emphasized by previous generations.

The bottom line indicates most people do not want to think about generational curses or universal challenges, let alone the implications and the impact of the previous generation upon the current generation. My conversations with my grandchildren have caused me to come to the realization that people generally just live for today. People give little serious thought to how their choices affect their future. Consequently, they certainly do not pay attention to the implication of yesterday's actions and (even more importantly) to the implication of today's actions!

NUMBER YOUR DAYS, MAKE EACH DAY COUNT

The simple reason Scripture encourages us to be mindful of our days is this, "we only get so many of them and then life is over".

Even so, people rarely stop to consider where they *could* be fifty years from now. For most young people, "life issues" have not become a concern, so how important today's decisions truly *are* has not clicked for them. Today always impacts tomorrow.

For a few moments, come back with me to my grandson Keaton who told me he would never let the dysfunctional things he encountered growing up influence his future life. At the start of our battle board sessions four and half years ago, none of us knew there would be a divine delay in the writing of this book which allowed Keaton time to gain new perspective on his battle and strategy. For Keaton, it turned out that one of his challenges would be identifying and overcoming his tendency to procrastinate. (I have his permission to share this.)

When I hosted that battle board session, he had no idea that his tendency to delay was a symptom of being impacted by dysfunction. Growing up in two very different yet loving homes, living with two different families, and having different rules for each household presented its own set of challenges. One home was more structured, and one home was more lenient, but given the choice what child would not prefer the easier road? But, in taking the easy road, it became easy to procrastinate, easy to delay, and easy to avoid taking action.

Keaton said, "I had grown up barely having to do anything—that was my normal. I had allowed myself to put things off and that too was my normal. But man, when I got to college, I suffered the consequences of never learning how to take action, make decisions, or avoid delay. I struggled because I was in this pattern of delay when presented with assignments and deadlines. My response would be 'yeah, I will do it. I can do that, I will do that', but then *I did not do it*. And I was not even aware that I had a problem, so I messed up my first couple of years. When I learned about this thing called "learned helplessness", it changed my world. I began to question why I was not getting anything done. And it dawned on me that I was not getting anything done because I was not doing anything."

Keaton went on to say, "So, I began to take ownership of my life. In doing that, I realized that I had to be actively active in my own betterment; actively active in my own happiness. I had to do it! No one else could, would, or should do it for me. That was the turning point of defeating the procrastination that had hindered my growth for far too long. Now, it is as simple as knowing that if I want to make an A this semester (and I do), it is not going to happen if I do not actively study; if I do not actively do the things I need to do to get that A."

FORGIVENESS STARTS WITH YOU

In a recent discussion regarding our past battle board session, Keaton just laughed and said, "I thought I knew everything back then! But now I know, I only knew in part. And the most important thing I have learned in this lesson of identifying and overcoming my procrastination tendency is that it is so important to forgive myself and to forgive others often because life is not a one-time event—it is a long journey. We are going to rise and fall all along the way, but we get back up so much faster when we commit to being open and honest with ourselves and each other."

As Keaton mentioned the word, "forgiveness" I could not help but think about some of my own family members and the impact they had upon me in my formative years. Though I knew those family members to be wonderful, loving, and kind, in retrospect, I realized that some of their actions were not wonderful, loving, and kind. God forbid I should ever emulate actions centered on bias, racism, and unforgiveness. I can look back now and just imagine what hardships those actions must have brought into their lives because, when you keep all that "stuff" inside of you, it creates more bitterness in you than it ever does in the person who is the target of your ugliness.

I have tried to instill into the lives of my grandchildren the belief that, if you are mad at someone because they have done something harmful to you, the best course of action by far is to act with forgiveness. Unforgiveness functions much like a cancer—it can consume you before you even know it's in your body. I believe that unforgiveness is one of the most powerful triggers of generational sins which stir up those universal challenges and pass them down from one generation to the next. We should be diligent when it comes to rooting out bitterness and harboring *unforgiveness*; it can stop you dead in your tracks and hold you back from ever reaching your potential. God forbid that we lose sight of this.

WEAPONS OF SELF DESTRUCTION

I have lived a good long life and over the years I have come to understand that when you become a Christian your sins are forgiven (past, present and future) and the curses are canceled. Yet, demonic spiritual forces are still active. Though they cannot possess one that belongs to the Lord, they can and do oppress! So, in that sense, we all have our demons—meaning there are spiritual forces that work against us in our vulnerabilities by driving certain issues that plague and weaken us to control certain aspects of our lives. An example might help.

My precious father was a hardworking man and was always the sole provider for our family. But each night when he would come home, his routine was to always have a couple of beers. Those couple of beers every night eventually evolved into drinking from 5-9 PM most evenings. Though he was never "drunk", he was a drinker. Can you hear "the cat's in the cradle with the silver spoon" playing in the background now? The habit of drinking beer night after night has been passed from one too many generations to the next. And yes, we have been *robbed* of *conversations we could have had* and *memories we could have made,* if only the beer habit had been broken.

My mother's family had their demons too. My mother had five brothers and some of them became excessive drinkers which eventually claimed their lives way too early. As for my uncles, they were raised in Kentucky during the years when Kentucky was a "dry" state—making and drinking "moonshine" was just a way of life. Alcohol became their entertainment. All five of my Uncles served in either WW1 or WW2, they were great Americans. Still, the saddest part of all was their unawareness of an ever-growing dependency to the drink that would enslave them and take them out of this world long before we were ready to say goodbye.

THE ELEPHANT IN THE ROOM PERSPECTIVE

WHY does this *happen* and WHAT is the *root* of all this dysfunction? There is always a lot of blame to go around. Really, the answer is simple: we find it easier to *settle* for IMITATION to cure ... what can only be *satisfied* by REAL. It has been that way since the snake first led us to doubt God ... Only what He offers truly satisfies and cures.

Addiction, dysfunction, co-dependency—all three trap our souls—creep so subtly and seemingly innocently into our lives. Often, what begins as something as harmless as taking a necessary prescribed pain pill becomes a raging addiction. I have seen it all.

A friend must have wisdom teeth extracted, receives a prescription for the pain, and before long is looking for the next fix. Next, the move from doctor to doctor to doctor begins because life is no longer livable without that next pain pill. While this may seem like an oversimplification, this is exactly how many people who struggle with drug addiction became addicted. It becomes a vicious cycle, far too often perpetuated from one generation to the next. What momma does, daughter does. What daddy does, son does. And the beat of self-destruction goes on. *Why,* you ask?

One seemingly harmless drink leads to the next. One seemingly sufficient drug leads to the next. One codependent relationship leads to the next. One affair leads to the next. One dogma leads to the next. One narcissistic behavior leads to the next. Need I say more?

Why will one family member act just like the previous generation, while a sibling does not? Honestly, I am not sure anyone knows the answer to that question. This I do know nothing is ever going to change if we are not willing to talk about our "issues," our "challenges," and those "generational curses" that clearly do continue from one generation to the next.

We must be willing to address *the elephant in the room.* We must be able to make a safe place for people to open up and talk about the things that have broken their hearts, shattered their dreams, and devastated their lives.

DECISIONS, DECISIONS, DECISIONS

Over the last four and a half years, I have watched my grandchildren identify their challenges, bring them out into the open, and deal with them head on. I am proud of who they are becoming.

Earlier, I mentioned my precious Ciera. Now there is grandchild that is finding her wings and is beginning to soar. Even as I wrote this chapter, she packed her bags and headed to Africa. She went to a place she had never been ... to meet children she had never met ... who were dealing with the emotional pain of abandonment. She knew their story only too well. Yet, Ciera had found her brave and there is no stopping her now. It is hard to describe how far she has come.

She told a friend of mine, "Because I lost my normal—a home with a mother and father (because they had issues that just did not allow for them being full time parents), I found myself always a bit scared. I had a wonderful grandmother that took over and did everything in her power to make life good for us, but I still wanted normal and I wanted normal for my brother and my sister. I wanted to make it okay for them when I saw their pain. So, I tried to be what they needed because I wanted them to be happy."

"But I had this huge awareness that *everything matters in life* (maybe because being left by my parents felt like the rug had been pulled out from under my feet) so I became afraid to make decisions ... even decisions as small as starting and completing a homework assignment. So, I would put it off until late in the evening, then I would be late getting to bed, then late waking up, then late to school and sometimes, honestly, I just did not get things done. There was always this tendency to delay because I was so nervous, so scared I would not do it right, and so I would just put it off."

She continued to share, "But one time I had this project; it was a paper that I had to write. I put it off as long as I could, but once I got started, I became super excited because it was really fun to write that paper. And I began to wonder, 'Why did it take me so long to decide to do something I really loved like writing?' Eventually, I discovered that the reason I felt such intense anxiety is because I did not really know myself well enough to answer my own questions.

DECIDE TO TELL A NEW STORY

With the help of a great therapist and the writings of Brené Brown, I am learning now to embrace my imperfections as gifts. And I am not hesitating near as much ... because I am learning who I am and Whose I am. God really loves me, and He has a plan for my life ... even the painful places will be part of God's story for my life."

You are not a loser, not disloyal, not hypocritical, not lazy, and not "not enough" when you are hesitant or afraid to take a courageous step towards doing what is right "next". You are normal. You are needed. You are a difference-maker.

We all live in a world fallen away from *the perfect relationship we were designed to live with God.* We know that every family has issues and that is certainly true of ours. It is why we are writing our story. We are hoping, as we share our story of learning how to be open and honest about the dysfunctions we have identified within our family, that you will find the courage to create an environment where it is safe to tell the truth. It will not always be easy, it may ruffle a few feathers, but with a big dose of grace you might be surprised at the transformation that is waiting for you as you gather your family around a table of love and choose to start telling the truth. Go for it! It could very well be the best thing you have ever done.

For whatever it may be worth to you, here are some words of encouragement right from our hearts to yours:

WHATEVER IT TAKES,

WHATEVER TIME IT TAKES,

DECIDE TO DO IT.

Defeating Generational Dysfunction, Finding Generational Freedom
Three Empowering Principles with Three Equipping Questions to Fight FOR YOUR FAMILY

CHAPTER TWO

Principle One. We do not know what we do not know, but God does.

Scripture: 1 Corinthians 1:25 (GNT) "...what seems to be God's foolishness is wiser than human wisdom, and what seems to be God's weakness is stronger than human strength."

Explanation: What we think is normal is always at best partial. The Good News is that God knows everything. God knows what you need to know. We are not asking for a download of everything—we would be totally overwhelmed. No one likes to admit that. We need to exchange what we have been *told* and have *perceived* for what is in reality...true. When we do, the elephant in the room is not scary like a bad dream—instead, it becomes an example that leads to healing.

Question 1.

To us, normal is often convenient and common. How will you sacrificially shift to "whatever it takes"?

Question 2.

When you have sacrificed for a long while, what will you say when you are asked for "more time"?

Question 3.

Since perspective may be shared (but is rarely matching), how will you choose to work together?

Principle Two. Forgiveness is a decision that precedes a feeling.

Scripture: Luke 23:34 (NIV) "Jesus said, 'Father, forgive them, for they do not know what they are doing.'"

Explanation: While hanging on the cross, Jesus offered His example to follow. In excruciating pain, He did not let how He felt cause Him to blame, condemn, or become bitter. He remembered how we use our limitations as excuses, and intentionally decided to demonstrate how to forgive. Wisdom decides to walk away from a prison before walking in. Withholding forgiveness is like walking into a jail cell and locking the door behind you. Decide to forgive before you feel like it.

Question 1.

People worry more about being *hypocritical* than about being *disobedient*. God commands us to forgive and tells us He will not forgive us unless we forgive. What will you surrender to forgive?

Question 2.

What else have you refused to do, then chosen to do, then wished you had done earlier? Why is change for the better challenging to you?

Question 3.

God tells us that, when we obey Him, we prove we love Him. How does forgiving someone prove your love (your commitment to lasting relationship)?

Principle Three. We must decide our future and our story.

Scripture: Deuteronomy 30:19-20 (NIV) "I have set before you life and death, blessings and curses. Now choose life, so that you and your children may live and that you may love the Lord your God, listen to his voice, and hold fast to him. For the Lord is your life, and He will give you many years..."

Explanation: God offers each of us an opportunity to choose life. The daily choices we make affect those around us far more than we realize. The first choice is to agree that each of us have contributed to the hole we have dug for ourselves. The second choice is to agree that God can fill the hole as we give Him that opportunity and as we let Him use us to make all of us better than we would have been otherwise. New chapters are the beginnings of the best endings.

Question 1.

We will never get different results if we continue to do the same thing or think the same way. What holes have you helped to dig that you want to close once and for all? What personal ideas and attitudes will you have to reject to have a new future and story for you and your family?

Question 2.

When will you sit down and begin to describe in writing the kind of future and life you desire? How will you love God enough to listen for His plan in the process?

Question 3.

What are you willing do to have a fresh start? How will you communicate your commitment to those who are closest to you?

Gary and Francie

Chapter Three
TELL THE TRUTH THAT HEALS

For as long as I can remember I have been fascinated with the subject of "communication." Having been a student of this subject matter for many decades, I am more resolutely convinced than ever that everything rises and falls upon the issue of communication. Impulsive and reckless communication has been the match that has lit a thousand flames of misunderstanding and has been the cause of unnecessary grief and untold heartbreak.

But, to wield the sword of healing truth-telling is more powerful, and more loving than we can imagine. It gives birth to new beginnings and fresh possibilities, unleashing power within to gloriously pursue God's dream for our lives. Yes! I am a huge proponent of good communication.

NO HEALING WITHOUT TRUTH

My pastor, Dr. Ed Young, has long underscored the fact that if a husband and a wife are committed to sitting down and talking calmly, peacefully, and in a loving manner about anything and everything—they will be able to work out differences that may exist. It may not be the answer they want, but issues can be resolved or a least managed in an agreeable healthy compromise every time and in every situation ... if good communication is an active part of their lives.

Every time I think about the subject of communication, I cannot help but think about some very dear friends of mine—one of the sweetest couples I have ever known. Sadly, their story poignantly illustrates the necessity of mutual communication—always and forever. The need for good communication never stops. Without it, relationships fail time and time again.

This couple (who Mike and I have known forever and dearly love) had a love story we thought would never end—not in a million years. I am telling you nothing seemed too difficult or too challenging for those two lovebirds—even when they attended separate colleges, nothing could come between them. He thought no one could hold a candle to his girl. And she thought the sun and the moon rose in his eyes. Theirs was true love and so they married right after college.

As the years went by, she continued to look up to the boy she fell in love with and depended on his leadership in their relationship. In fact, she never made a decision without checking in with her husband. It was all she had ever known since they were young teenagers. She placed him on such a high pedestal and allowed him to make every decision. Innocently, in doing so, they never learned to participate, as a couple, in the healthy give-and-take decision-making process that is so necessary for a marriage to thrive. And so, when her husband experienced a mid-life crisis and found it difficult to make quick and easy decisions, their love story began to unravel. As time went on, things grew worse as even the simplest things would take months to decide, because he could not make up his mind.

As one might assume, this eventually became a great point of contention in their relationship. Then, when they discovered that one of their children had an addiction issue, things became even more difficult. The wife felt that, no matter how much she tried to communicate with him the seriousness of their child's issues, her husband would not hear what she had to say. And he felt that his wife was making too much of the problem and that it would all blow over in time and their child would be fine. But her husband was struggling with a mid-life-crisis and an inability to make decisions. He could not sit down to talk about it, nor would he accept that his child was in deep trouble.

The wife wanted desperately for her husband to take the bull by the horns and just say, "We have got a problem, and this is how we are going to solve it." But he could not. He had been stuck in the pattern of non-decision making for so long and, because they had never learned how to sit down and talk through issues together as a couple, they found themselves in a terrible mess.

She tried everything she knew how to do. Eventually, she decided she could no longer live with the stress, anxiety, and weight of it all. That beautiful love story came needlessly to an end all because they had never learned to mutually communicate in all matters of the heart. If only they had learned from the very beginning the secret that *everything rises and falls upon great communication.*

BEGIN THE HEALING HABIT

I do not know why I was so incredibly blessed to have had parents that taught me from a very early age the importance of honest truth-telling communication. But for whatever reason, I did have that kind of parents and I will forever be grateful because children learn how to communicate by watching our communication skills. When I was growing up, my parents insisted that if my brother and I wanted to be listened to "to be heard", then we must learn how to kindly and respectfully listen to others "to understand and respond".

When my brother and I were growing up, there were not many children in our lives to interact with, but there were always a lot of adults. We lived in Texas and our extended family lived in Michigan. When the Michigan family came to visit, most of them were older and did not have children tagging along. But my brother and I were always excited to see them and, even if there were no children, we wanted to be a part of the conversation. So, my parents insisted that if we were going to be in the room and a part of the conversation, then we had to learn to "*listen*" to what others were saying. As a result, the listening and communication skills training I received came unusually early in life, but it has served me very, very well.

What my parents did to create an environment that was conducive to good communication was far better than any college course could have ever offered. They took the time to sit with us at the dinner table and talk with us and they included us in the conversation when company came to our home. So, when I grew up and became a parent within a blended family, it became all the more important to emulate the wonderful practice of teaching my children how to *listen well* in order that they might *be heard* and more importantly become a worthy contributor to conversations that take place within the home and ultimately in the world at large.

HEALING IS A CHOICE

Now, with that being said, trying to introduce my core conviction regarding communication was not always easy in the beginning days of our blended family. The merging of two different ways of doing things naturally presented a bit of a challenge. For example, my husband's boys had spent their young years enjoying dinner in front of the television and they were quick to tell us that the new way of enjoying dinner around the family table—talking and sharing conversation—was not as enjoyable to them as their old way. So, for a while, it was a tug-of-war to get them to learn to embrace a new way doing dinner, sharing life around the family table.

Perhaps it was the *challenges* of the blended family life that strengthened my resolve to communicate in creative and supportive ways that would help my family, especially the children feel loved and connected, despite divorce. I understand that today divorce is common. My family is no exception. But nonetheless, I never wanted anyone in my family to feel left out. The unforeseen result is my extended family has continued to become increasingly important to me. It is so important that I have done some things that some people find quite *peculiar*, but I find quite *freeing*.

HEALING IS A CHOICE TO LOVE

Let me explain. My husband, Mike, was divorced twice before we married, and I was divorced once. But what many find surprising is this: I invited the ex-wives and my ex-husband to our wedding and have subsequently invited them to almost every family gathering and social affair we have ever hosted. In the beginning, many of my friends were often shocked to see these individuals in my home. However, this is something the grandchildren have grown to appreciate. The lesson they have learned is that, in our family, being divorced from a former spouse does not mean that the children are divorced from other family members of their extended family. Even the extended families of the divorced spouses are invited to our family-oriented events. It is what we do ... and it started the day Mike and I said, "I do."

We were married in an outdoor wedding and all our children were part of the wedding as little groomsmen and bridesmaids. Whenever I look back at those pictures, I am convinced this was the absolute best way to start our marriage because the children felt so connected. They had their grandparents, great-grandparents, and other extended family members there from both sides of the family. On that day, I knew beyond a shadow of doubt, I was not just marrying Mike, I was marrying them all. The truth is I chose to love the whole extended family!

One year after our marriage in 1977, the Brady Bunch became a hit television show. It was quite sappy and perhaps surreal because of how they *portrayed* the "blended family" as always happy, all the time. For those of us living with and dealing with the real issues of a blended family, the show proved to be quite unrealistic. But, one important theme that was consistent in that show was that they always worked out their conflicts and differences because they communicated and talked about their problems. They told the truth that heals.

THE HEALING TRUTH IS RARE

Back then, in the early days of our marriage, I do not think the term "blended family" even existed. I cannot even begin to tell you how many times I went looking for books about how to put two families together. I could not find more than two books on the subject. However, bookstores and libraries are now full of books on this subject. Yet, I have found that very few people have done what Mike and I have done regarding bringing our families together.

Maybe we were ahead of our time. I do not know. But this is what I do know because I have lived long enough to see it play out time and time again: *Truth-telling helps and heals.*

Honest, deep, real, and true communication plays such an important role in our lives and it affects every single relationship in our lives. If you have not been around good communication, it is likely your communication skills are lacking. If that is the case, take heart because you are not alone. Our society is filled with individuals who do not know how to effectively communicate. When it comes to communication, there is one thing for certain (the best communicators will tell you this): miscommunication is inevitable, but it does not ever have to be the end. Truthful communication can be learned by anyone who has the heart to seek and speak the truth. I have seen this happen in my own family in the lives of my children and grandchildren.

LOVE MUST TELL THE TRUTH THAT HEALS

Let me tell you a story—a real story brimming with hope that anyone can learn to become a truth-telling communicator.

My son's family is "as tight as tight can be". His children are fiercely loyal to one another and it is a beautiful thing to see. It is really refreshing in a world where sibling rivalry can often be vicious and ugly—not so in their family. These siblings would do just about anything to keep one another out of trouble. And that is where this story begins.

Years ago, back when they were still in high school his oldest daughter lost her way for just a bit. His middle child adored her big sister. Truth be known, early on she probably thought her big sister walked on water. Early on, she would do just about anything for her big sister, even if it meant telling a few "harmless" white lies.

The only problem was that, the more lost her big sister became, the little sister's heart began to experience great conflict. More than anything in the world that little sister wanted to be "the good sister, the cool sister, the one who would never do anything to break her big sister's heart." So, she stayed silent, even though she questioned "Is what my sister doing normal for a teenager?"

The long story made short—that little sister found the courage to become a healing truth-teller. It was the hardest thing she had ever done. She not only opened up to her parents, but she wrote her sister an intervention letter telling her sister how she really felt. Read this carefully: she spelled out the truth in black and white holding nothing back. Her big sister later said, "It was *the meanest thing* I ever read, but it was also *the one thing* that made me want to change."

I wish you could see these two girls now. Well, they are not girls anymore—they are beautiful young women and they are fierce communicators. It was not easy to speak the truth in love, but it has become a hallmark in their lives.

ALLI: HANDING DOWN GENERATIONAL BLESSINGS

Four and half years ago when I first sat down with the grandchildren to talk battle board strategies for overcoming their greatest possible future challenges, my granddaughter Alli just blew me away.

We were talking about marriage because, even though Alli was an outstanding college student and holds high aspirations of becoming a highly paid executive in the traditional work-force, her deepest desire has always been to be an outstanding wife and mother, perhaps especially because Alli's parents have had their share of challenges over the years. This granddaughter loves everything family! She wants a home of her own, a husband to love, and children to raise.

In the course of our conversation, I asked Alli "What do you think will keep your marriage from having some of the same difficulties and challenges as your parent's marriage? What, if anything, do you think is lacking in the marriage?" Without missing a heartbeat, she quickly said, "Communication." I nearly fell off my chair when I heard her insightful response. For a long time now, I have talked about communication to all my grandchildren and its importance in relationships. But I was still *stunned* by her response.

So, I probed a little deeper, brought it in a little closer to home, and asked, "Do you have an easy time communicating with your boyfriend?" She said, "Yes, we talk about everything." I then asked, "What kind of ups and downs have you had and how have you solved them?" She confidently responded, "Mia, we just sit down, and I tell him what I did not like, and he tells me what he did not like." I said "Alli that is huge! Ninety-nine percent of the time people side-step what they do not like and actually talk about other things that are not even pertinent to the issue at hand because they do not *know how to say* what they really do not like." I thought her response was such a mature answer.

Alli went on to admit that *it is not always fun to communicate, and I totally agree.* Truth-telling, tough-love-speaking communication is not always enjoyable; it is not always fun. There will be times when you will have to speak about the worst possible things, and it will not be fun and may even break your heart. Like, when a husband comes home and confesses to his wife that he had an affair and tries to explain why he did it—no wife is going to be happy to hear that her husband has broken the sacred trust of marriage.

I shared with Alli, "My observation has been that the top three major issues that seem to plague a marriage are money, immediate and extended family, and extra-marital affairs. These are the top reasons for people eventually fall into the divorce-mindset. These issues are so personal and emotionally driven that they often *seem* difficult (if not impossible) to talk about."

I then asked Alli, "Do you think you could talk to your spouse about things like that?" She said, "If it meant I was going to save my marriage I could." "Well, what if you did not like his answer?" I questioned. "Well, Mia," she said, "That's why therapists have jobs. If we cannot settle it and make it right when we talk, then we need to go to someone to get help. We need to find either someone at our church or a therapist or someone that will sit down with us. I can tell you story after story about many of my friends who have broken up over senseless things. And they were "senseless" things because they were never willing to talk about it."

TURN RIGHT ONTO HEALING ROAD

Alli's battle board words four and half years ago all centered on *great communication*. Today, her battle board words are still the same. By her own admission she is a hopeless romantic. However, her firm grasp on an ever-growing conviction on the importance of great communication continues to define her life. The obstacles and challenges she has faced have absolutely shaped her opinions and made her vigilant in her pursuit of being a straight shooter. And if I may be so bold, let me just say, "She is a confident woman who knows how to brilliantly communicate what she believes, and she does it in a non-threatening, non-judgmental way."

Like when she just straight up says "Umm, 'No!' That's not the truth!" to all the men in the Willis family who swear that "driving fast and getting tickets" is in their blood because it has been passed down from grandfather to dad to son. She just rolls her eyes and they know she knows *"They are telling the truth...NOT!"*

I'm proud of this girl who has learned so much in such a short time that "the road to healing begins" when we are willing to bring things out of the dark and into the light. She knows, because she has learned with every heartache (one of her own or one of her family members') that what we cannot see ... we cannot change, but what we can see—what we are willing to bring into the light—we absolutely can change and the truth *does not hurt*, it helps and heals.

Defeating Generational Dysfunction, Finding Generational Freedom
Three Empowering Principles with Three Equipping Questions to Fight FOR YOUR FAMILY

CHAPTER THREE

Principle One. We can participate in one another's wholeness and healing.

Scripture: James 5:16 (MSG) "Make this your common practice: Confess your sins to each other and pray for each other so that you can live together whole and healed. The prayer of a person living right with God is something powerful to be reckoned with."

Explanation: Confession is countercultural; it feels vulnerable and unsafe. Biblically, confession says to God "I was wrong, and You are right". We are not unique, in that we all have reason to confess, to pray together, and ask God to heal us. Confession requires careful search for trustworthy hearers who will pray with wisdom and compassion. Begin with those mistakes you have a part in, knowing that our prayers for one another could be far more powerful than we know.

Question 1.

What keeps you from saying "I was wrong"? What will it take for you to say those words?

Question 2.

Why is it challenging for families to pray: "God, help us to lay down our pride and say what is true."?

Question 3.

According to this verse, what power do families miss when they will not take these simple steps?

Principle Two. We can be free when we love each other enough to speak truth.

Scripture: John 8:31-32 (MSG) "Then Jesus turned to the Jews who had claimed to believe in Him. 'If you stick with this, living out what I tell you, you are My disciples for sure. Then you will experience for yourselves the truth, and the truth will free you.'"

Explanation: It is one thing to be aware of what is true and simply agree. There is value in knowing who is willing to tell us the truth, then loves us enough and cares enough to take the risk. This level of encouragement causes us to get past knowing about the truth and get to the place where we are willing to do the truth to experience its power to set us free. Love is not just an emotional *feeling*—much more than that, love is powerful *action* that makes a lifechanging difference.

Question 1.

Is there anyone who is more believable than God? What keeps you from believing Him?

Question 2.

How long are you willing to keep telling the truth in a loving way?

Question 3.

How committed are you to experiencing Truth that *frees* you and your family?

Principle Three. We need one another to grow into a healthy loving family.

Scripture: Ephesians 4:15-16 (NLT) "Instead, we will speak the truth in love, growing in every way more and more like Christ, who is the head of His body, the church. He makes the whole body fit together perfectly. As each part does its own special work, it helps the other parts grow, so that the whole body is healthy and growing and full of love."

Explanation: God is interested in the eternal quality of your daily life. His commitment begins with now and extends into the eternal quantity of your future. It is safe to say that becoming more like Christ means we become healthy effective parts of one another's lives. We are needed contributors to one another's growth and sense that we are committed to one another's abundance and destiny. We do need one another. We do matter to God's plan for every one of us.

Question 1.

If *the most common thought in conflict resolution* is "you don't need me", what can change that thought pattern?

Question 2.

Why are you needed in your family's healing? What do you bring to the table that *no one else does?*

Question 3.

How do you *see your family growing* over years to come? How will its future change *because of your choices?*

Chapter Four
GET WHAT YOU "DON'T" DESERVE

I hate bullying! I not only hate it for what it is—I hate it for what it does. Bullying causes people to judge themselves without mercy.

WHAT NO ONE DESERVES

What I hate even more is that most times bullying is inflicted upon the most innocent of souls—our children. They come into the world so full of life, with a sparkle in their eyes that is unmatched anywhere this side of heaven. Theirs is a future brimming with promise, a life unmarred by the unkindness and cruelty of others. But it is only for a brief season.

Before we know it, little souls get busted and broken. Children get labeled and stamped with stigmas often inflicted through bullying. Self-limiting beliefs are soon implanted within their minds. If left uncontested, self-limiting beliefs become rooted in the wounded hearts of children and follow them throughout every season of their lives. They steal children's joy and eventually have the power to strip them of their true identity.

The Scripture says that it is the enemy who comes "to steal and kill and destroy."[6] Wound a soul deeply enough through a bully-imposed self-limiting belief and that creation of God may never know how wonderfully gifted He has made them. They reach adulthood believing *they do not deserve any better*, they do not deserve to flourish and thrive, and they do not deserve to enjoy the gifts that are within them. All they have ever known or remember are the lies that have been spoken over them—lies they have surrendered to embrace. And so, *they judge themselves without mercy.*

EVERYONE DESERVES A SAFE PLACE

But there comes a time when each one of us must learn to say, *"Enough is enough!"* The ultimate goal of bullying is to demean and demoralize another human being. *It must stop!*

At its core, bullying seeks to put a person in their "place" and that *place* is always beneath the boot of the one doing the bullying. Saddest of all is the fact that bullying does not just happen in our schools. It happens every day in our homes, workplaces, relationships, and even in our churches.

Bullying at home happens when a child is subjected to repeated forms of verbal, physical and/or emotional abuse. Bullying in the workplace happens when an employee is subjected to repeated public and/or private humiliation from a superior who misuses their position of authority. Bullying in a relationship happens when an individual seeks to force their will upon another human being through manipulation, browbeating, and/or through the onslaught of verbal, physical and emotional abuse. Bullying in a church happens when spiritual people twist and manipulate the Word of God for selfish gain. They heap condemnation upon those entrusted to their care and remind them often how much they fail to please God.

In these environments of dysfunction, self-limiting beliefs take root, and the one impacted by the dysfunction begins to believe that they do not deserve *to live full.* So, *they judge themselves without mercy.* They hang their heads in shame. They never *dare* to believe they are worthy of something more, something greater than the humiliation that has been daily dripped or indifferently dumped upon their souls. Even worse, in the dark they whisper, "Lord, have mercy! What if these people knew how bad I really am—they would never want to know me then. Because they would know they are right—I do not deserve any better. *I am without worth.*"

THE COMMONPLACE SCENARIO

Regrettably, I have seen the devastating effects of a bully-imposed self-limiting belief on more than one occasion. It is all too *commonplace.*

I know a sweet young boy who comes from a divorced home. He spends half of his time with his mother and the other half with his daddy (as if that isn't hard enough.) When he was very little, he attended pre-school and kindergarten at a Montessori school. The Montessori educational model encouraged him to learn in whatever manner felt comfortable to him. If he wanted to stand up, he could stand up. If he wanted to walk to the other side of the room, he had the liberty to do so. That model of education was very different from the public-school system's model of education where students experienced a much more structured routine. Consequently, it was a painful and difficult transition for that child when he had to enter the highly controlled environment of the public-school system.

He was consistently singled out by the teacher and experienced a variety of disciplines to correct his "seemingly misaligned" behavior. As a result, that little boy who was once so full of joy became the "outsider" in the classroom. He became a target for ridicule by other classmates and was often subjected to bullying. His classmates saw him as "different", teased him incessantly, and did not want to have anything to do with him.

Remarkably, that wonderful little boy (who was rejected and abandoned as the other children withheld their friendship) has learned to overcome past patterns with new coping skills that neutralize abusive comments and behaviors. Summarized well, he says with words and actions, "Bug off!"

Mercifully, that child that has been subjected to bullying chooses not to bully in return. He is an overcomer!

COMMONPLACE IS UNACCEPTABLE

How does this type of behavior begin at such an early age? It seems that it does not take much of a reason for one child to dislike another. Today, some children are already looking at the clothes another child is wearing to determine if that child qualifies to be "accepted" into the "friend" group. And if a child does not look or act like everyone else, that child will likely be bullied, pushed, shoved, tripped, and deliberately be made to look like a buffoon. Before long, *but for the intervention of God, that child will judge himself without mercy.*

I have a grandson who is extremely smart (well ... truthfully, I think they are all brilliant). But he was the kid in the classroom who would always be the first to raise his hand in response to the teacher's questions because he always knew the answers. It happened so often that the teacher would have to bypass my grandson's raised hand to give other students in the class a chance to answer her questions.

One day, after school had been in session for a couple of months, my grandson, with his lunch tray in hand, sat down at a table with four other boys. As soon as he sat down, the other four boys stood up and took their lunch trays to a different table. A teacher saw this happen and called the four boys into a conference later that day. She asked them, "Why did you all get up when that young man sat down at your table?" They responded, "We do not want to sit with him." She immediately replied, "Well, that's totally inappropriate and in the future, you will sit with him." While the kind-hearted teacher was trying to do the right thing, her seating requirement made it very uncomfortable for my grandson.

Making matters even worse, the next day the mother of one of the boys who were reprimanded came to the school and told the principal what had happened with the teacher the previous day. That mother was not happy. She informed the principal that she was not going to pay tuition for her son to attend the school only to be miserable during his lunch period because he was being forced to sit with someone with whom he did not care to sit. This was a fourth-grade student! It was obvious to see where the student obtained his disposition regarding who would and who would not be accepted. They say that apples do not fall far from the tree.

It was deplorable for that mother to reinforce the degrading behavior of her child. But truth is, probably all adults and parents have displayed behaviors for which they are not proud, or which could potentially have a negative impact on their children. No doubt we have all been guilty of less than exemplary behavior. Unfortunately, countless children have seen their parents and other family members model dysfunctional actions that are unhealthy, hurtful and, in some cases, even disgraceful. Like the damage that was inflicted upon my grandson with parental support, the ramifications of modeling for our children the dysfunctional behavior of demeaning others has far reaching consequences.

Thankfully, the principal did not agree with the mother and gave the four boys detention that week for their shameful misconduct in the lunchroom. The principal's diplomacy in this matter of the mistreatment of my grandson was remarkable. While he did not make the four boys sit with my grandson, they were told that once they were seated, they were not to move to another table—no matter who came to sit there. Though the principal's response was appropriate, unfortunately no one wanted to sit with my grandson at lunch from that time forward.

My grandson would get in the car after school and burst into tears. He did not understand why he was being rejected—no child would. He would tell his mom how sad he was because his classmates did not want to talk to him, sit with him, or play with him at recess. His teacher made a concerted effort to correct this problem as the school year progressed by encouraging children to interact with him. But sadly, he experienced more isolation, because no one wanted him.

Is it any wonder why so many people *struggle to know their worth? I'm betting that the wounded heart of a child still beats within the chests of many people.* Many are never able to reverse the stigmas that have been imposed upon them through the dysfunctional behavior of others.

The self-limiting belief that has taken root in their soul often results in life lived in isolation. They never feel worthy of love and so they come to believe that they truly do not deserve better.

Stuck in the mindset of unworthiness, they simply "suck it up" and trudge through life.

THE UNCOMMON PLACE OF MERCY AND GRACE

Some do not know that their heavenly Father loves them and stands ready to pour grace upon grace into their lives. Some know the fact of the Father's love yet are unable to receive the experience of it. Regrettably, some never recover from the self-limiting beliefs that have been heartlessly heaped upon their souls.

If we are to hope for a better future for those we love, then we are going to have to grapple with the intolerable behavior of belittling and berating others who simply may not be like us. We must talk openly and honestly with our children about the way we must treat other people. Today we see the far-reaching effects, in our society, of disparaging others—we must not be satisfied with apathy residing in our homes! We must wrestle this issue to the ground and not relinquish the battle until these antagonistic behaviors are defeated in us.

It is within our ability to take spiritual authority over these destructive spirits that seek to divide and conquer us internally and relationally. For the health and prosperity of future generations, we need to be willing to identify and stand against all patterns of dysfunction that cause others to embrace a self-limiting belief. God has provided weapons of discernment and prayer that are available to us to destroy what is destroying us without destroying each other.

People must learn that they are worthy of love and deserve to thrive and flourish in all of life. It is absolutely within our power to make a difference in their lives. It takes unwavering commitment to treat others with respect and love on the basis that people are created in the image of God.

PERSONAL TRAGEDY, SOCIETY'S EPIDEMIC

Recently, I watched a tragic incident on a news channel that underscored the seriousness of imposing a self-limiting belief upon another individual through the cruelty of bullying. It broke my heart.

A father was being interviewed as he shared with reporters that his eighteen-year-old daughter had been a victim of cyber-bullying for about a year. The grief-stricken father choked out the story that his daughter had constantly received upsetting and relentless text messages (mostly about her weight) which were sent from a smart phone with an untraceable phone number. The news report quoted a family member as saying, "They would make dating websites for her, put her number and picture on the sites, lie about her age, and say she was giving herself up for sex for free. As a result, she was experiencing excruciating depression and anxiety." The family said they reported the bullying to the school district as well as several law enforcement agencies, but the response always the same: "There is nothing we can do anything about it."

Despite this young teen changing her phone number, the bullies somehow always found her. Then came the tragic day the family hoped would never come. She sent an email to all of her family members telling them she was going to take her own life. She sent a final text message that simply read, "I love you so much, just remember that please, and I am so sorry for everything." Her distressed family rushed home to find her with a gun plunged into her chest. The father was sure he could persuade his daughter to lay down the gun. But her pain was too great, and in the presence of her family she pulled the trigger and ended her life.

WHAT CAN BE DONE HAS BEEN DONE

As a mother and a grandmother, I cannot fathom this grief. Yet, this very real scenario is repeated over and over every year within our country. With the arrival of Facebook, Twitter, Instagram, Snap Chat and a host of other social media platforms, social and relational bullying is on the rise. There is a dangerous game being played and precious lives are at stake. When rumors are spread and lies are told for the purpose of deliberately damaging the reputation of another, there will always be a victim whose life may never recover from the malice inflicted by another demeaning human being. They struggle their whole lives, needlessly believing they are not worthy to be loved; needlessly continuing to judge themselves without mercy. That is beyond tragic.

Despite all that my grandson suffered; he has grown into a fine young man. He has recovered from those early wounds; wounds that were unnecessary. However, God redeemed those wounds and has shaped his life through those hard places. I beam with joy when I look at the man he is becoming. I have heard him on more than one occasion say, "We need to always be willing to try to see things from the other person's point of view."

Not only do I have a grandson who has faced bullying, I have a granddaughter who was confronted with horrible bullying during her high school years. With such amazing courage, she has defied a lot of pain and faced a lot of rejection. Time and time again, she has risen to the occasion, pushed through the heartache, and in the process gained a tremendous amount of confidence through hard work and multiple achievements.

Brittany once told me that she knew when she would be rejected, so she became hardened to the rejection and she also became wise to it. In becoming wise, she made the conscious decision to quit trying to be a part of certain groups because she realized she was not going to be accepted. And yes, her feelings were extremely hurt. Fortunately, for my granddaughter, the cyber-bullying was short lived, and she now enjoys many friendships. But I grieve for those who never find the courage to overcome the obstacle of self-limiting beliefs that bind a soul in unmerciful self-judgment.

It breaks my heart when I think of that little boy that cries because he has no friends, and the ridicule and rejection my own two grandchildren have had to endure. But here's the truth—in some form or fashion, we have all felt the sting of rejection, because we live in a fallen world.

We are a flawed people—every single one of us. We have known what it is like to feel the weight of unworthiness—to feel unloved and unwanted. But there is One Who would say to us, "Follow Me! I have got you covered. I will never seek to expose your flaws or single you out for humiliation. Never! Your past will not be the predictor of your future—because 'I know the plans I have for you. They are plans for good and not for disaster, to give you a future and a hope.'"[7]

When I look at my two grandchildren's ability to overcome the effects of dysfunction from those bully-imposed self-limiting beliefs, I see a picture of God's daily renewed mercy and all-sufficient grace in the difficulties of life. I see a God who wants to pour out His redemption upon all our messes and our muddles.

As my grandson Grayson likes to share, *"There is a verse that kind of just hits you in the heart. It is the verse that implies He still loves you—He still LOVES YOU! You may even now be doing something terrible—but, He still currently actively loves you!* He is not saying He only loves you if you do not you sin, He is not saying He only loves you if you're good—He is saying, right now in the middle of your mess, HE LOVES YOU! And we may be tempted to think (when we're really blowing it) "I don't know if He likes me right now", but here's *the real deal*, the verse says, He loves you right now and He is rooting for you!" This is the verse: "But this is how God demonstrates His own love for us: The Messiah died for us while we were still sinners."[8]

Over the years, I have come to understand that I do not have all the answers. But I do have to take ownership for the issues that I and my family may face. However, part of taking ownership is recognizing and acknowledging that many issues are much bigger than me. Some are way beyond my control.

So, I learned years ago that "the battle belongs to the Lord."[9] And the only way you will be able to get a grip on the issues that impact your family is to lay them at the feet of Jesus and allow Him to change your heart and your family. Allow Him to use you in resolving issues, but do not try to go it alone. Philippians 4:13 says, "I can do all things through Christ Who gives me strength."[10] I can do it and you can do it too—but only through Christ Who gives us strength and wisdom to accomplish it. If you do not allow the strength of Christ to work in and through you, it will only be an exercise in pure futility and it will leave you exhausted, frustrated, confused, and broken-hearted.

The bottom line is simply this: "All of us have sinned and fallen short of God's glory."[11] Because of that, we all have areas where we have embraced self-limiting beliefs. Therefore, there have been times that we have judged ourselves and others ruthlessly and without Mercy. *The truth of the matter is that none of us gets what we deserve.* But God Who is slow to anger and full of compassion gives us beautiful *Mercy* for our broken souls—*He does not give us what we do deserve.*

Instead, because of *what Jesus has done for us,* God has given us His grace and favor which we do not deserve. On a Cross long ago, it was Jesus' blood that paid for This Gift, which we do not deserve. WITH OUR WORDS, we can offer and extend favor, we are able to tell all those who live within the sphere of our influence about the love, mercy, and grace of God! And, that is how we can make an unstoppable difference in the lives of others, every day!

Today, may you and all that you love, cease to judge yourselves without mercy and may you know fully and completely that you are loved. The Father sees YOU complete in Him!

Defeating Generational Dysfunction, Finding Generational Freedom
Three Empowering Principles with Three Equipping Questions to Fight FOR YOUR FAMILY

CHAPTER FOUR

Principle One. We are all guilty of disregard of God. Yet, He willingly offers mercy. None of us deserve His best. Yet, He offers grace.

Scripture: Exodus 33:19 (NIV)

"I will have mercy on whom I will have mercy, and I will have compassion on whom I will have compassion. "

Scripture: Ephesians 2:8-9 (NIV) "For it is by grace you have been saved, through faith—and this not from yourselves, it is the gift of God—not by works, so that no one can boast."

Explanation: Sin is simply disregard for God. Sins are actions or inactions that show we disregard Him. Mercy is God's choice to *withhold what we do deserve* [punishment] because He is compassionate. Grace is His Choice to *give us what we do not deserve* [abundant life] because He loves us. His Love is not an emotional preference; it is a demonstration of His commitment to us forever. Jesus offers His Grace because He regards us and desires the very best for us.

Question 1.

What would life be like if we did not keep score based on how we feel, and instead we kept score on how compassionate we are towards others who are weak, hurting, failing, clueless, and lost?

Question 2.

Why is it challenging for us to accept mercy and grace? Why do we feel there is a catch? Why are we afraid to admit what we need and receive what we need?

Question 3.

Why would "living with one another in His mercy and grace" make life easier for you and for them?

Principle Two. We can admit that we need power, learn-how, and practice.

Scripture: Romans 5:6-8 (MSG) "Christ arrives right on time to make this happen. He didn't, and doesn't, wait for us to get ready. He presented Himself for this sacrificial death when we were far too weak and rebellious to do anything to get ourselves ready. And even if we hadn't been so weak, we wouldn't have known what to do anyway. We can understand someone dying for a person worth dying for, and we can understand how someone good and noble could inspire us to selfless sacrifice. But God put His love on the line for us by offering His Son in sacrificial death while we were of no use whatever to Him."

Explanation: If you think that God is waiting for you to muster up the brains and willpower to get it right, nothing could be farther from the truth. Instead, He is simply waiting for you to say you are ready for His power to learn and to put that learning into practice. That totally messes up what most people expect. God is not interested in what people deserve. He is interested in giving you the life that He created you to live, nothing more, nothing less. That life is better than you imagine.

Question 1.

You know there is more to life than this and people just seem to be interested in getting what they can while they can, no matter what. If what you have read so far is true, what is your first move?

Question 2.

What are you willing to do with your "don't deserve" and "do deserve" standards?

Question 3.

How will you put yourself and others on a level playing field where you all belong?

Principle Three. We need one another to grow into a healthy loving family.

Scripture: Hebrews 4:13-16 (NIV) "Nothing in all creation is hidden from God's sight. Everything is uncovered and laid bare before the eyes of Him to Whom we must give account. Therefore, since we have a great high priest Who has gone through the heavens, Jesus the Son of God, let us hold firmly to the faith we profess. For we do not have a high priest who is unable to sympathize with our weaknesses, but we have One Who has been tempted in every way, just as we are — yet was without sin. Let us then approach the throne of grace with confidence, so that we may receive mercy and find grace to help us in our time of need. "

Explanation: Since God sees everything and is The Only One, we are ultimately accountable to, we have a bigger agenda than daily survival. Because Jesus came to show us how to live on earth, He experienced every challenge and with its pain. Because of Him, we can confidently access grace we do not deserve to share healthy life with one another. God expects us to live the lives we were individually created to live to benefit one another—family first.

Question 1.

How will your thinking have to change to make your health (and family's health) your priority?

Question 2.

What kind of power from God will you need to change your way of thinking, being, and doing?

Question 3.

How will becoming a victor over your past change the way you live every day?

Chapter Five
CHOOSE TO BELIEVE LIFE CAN BE FULL OF JOY

If we know anything about Jesus, it is this: Jesus was not a *killjoy*. The gospel of John, chapter two, records that Jesus began His ministry celebrating at a wedding and turning water into wine. His first miracle was at a party! What a picture to paint for the world! His ministry began with celebration and joy—it was to say, right from the beginning, I have come so "that your joy may be made full and complete and overflowing."[12]

Like two magnificent bookends, not only does His ministry start with great joy, His ministry ends with great joy! Facing a most gruesome horrific death by crucifixion upon a cross, we read these words in the Holy Scriptures, "...for the joy that lay before Him, He endured the cross..."[13] He did not focus on the agony, or the suffering, or the shame of it all. In His greatest hour of need, Christ focused on the joy that was ahead for Him and for us!

I believe, without doubt, that is a clue as to how He would have us live our lives. Like Jesus, we too can choose to focus on the promised joy. Even when sorrow and suffering is present in our lives, we need to focus on the joy that is promised to us rather than fixate on our misery. And we do this best when we make a conscious effort to partner with others who take joy in finding breakthrough rather than commiserating with those who like to roll around in the mud of despair and distress. I have lived long enough to realize that misery loves company, but I have come to truly appreciate that joy loves partnership!

JOY IS WORTH SEEKING

I have had a front row seat to many of the heartaches of my children, my grandchildren, my employees, my associates, and my friends. And, I know that everyone goes through difficult times.

Yet, I know you would agree that it is much harder to watch your child or other children in your life suffer than it is for you to endure a sorrow. When they are hurting, we find ourselves wanting to take their place in a New York minute, yet it is not possible or best. Looking back and watching their journey into adulthood, I have seen God build something beautiful through those challenges and hard places. I would not take those learned lessons away from them for anything—those difficulties have shaped their lives, have made them resilient, and turned them into seekers of joy. O God, how I hope they never lose their joy!

I want to hold on ever so tightly to this hope that I have in my heart for my family! I so desperately want them to experience joy through every season of life—regardless of what life may throw their way.

I want them to be experience-driven rather than task-driven.

Now, do not miss the point of the truth I am telling. I want them to accomplish a lot with every resource God has placed in their precious lives! I want them to be productive. I want them to flourish. I want them to thrive, but NOT at the expense of sacrificing joy.

I do not want to see them become so task-driven that they miss the spontaneity of laughter-filled moments. I am standing in faith that they will know great joy and that their joy will be infectious in all of their spheres of influence. That is what I'm praying for and believing for my grandchildren, great niece and nephews—that they will know great joy!

JOY IS BELIEVING BEFORE SEEING

I want to think with you about faith but, while we do, I do not want to leave out joy. So, consider with me that the Word of God says this: "Now faith is the reality of what is hoped for, the proof of what is not seen."[14] I heard this story once that has really helped me to understand how I could practically live out this verse. Let me share it with you.

There was a father who had eleven children. His dream was to see all eleven children receive a college education. He did not know how he could possibly fund the college education for eleven children. But he knew that God had placed this dream in his heart, so he decided to stand in faith and believe God for their education. To demonstrate his faith, he hung eleven empty frames on the walls of his home. Every time someone would ask him "Why do you have eleven empty frames on your walls", he would smile and say, "The Good Book says, 'faith is the reality of what is hoped for, the proof of what is not *yet* seen.'[15] By faith, one day those eleven frames are going to hold eleven college diplomas! Those empty frames hanging on my walls are the evidence of things I have not yet seen which I believe shall surely come to pass because His Word declares "*with God all things are possible.*"[16] Those frames are my visible reminder that God will make a way."

I BELIEVE

I love that story because I have a picture that I'm holding onto! It is a picture that does for me what those empty frames did for that father. Several years ago, I took what should be considered an award-winning photograph of two of my grandsons who are brothers and best of friends. In the photo, one of my grandsons is telling a story (probably a tall tale, if the truth was known) and his brother is sitting next to him with his head flung fully back and laughing the biggest belly laugh ever. It is priceless! It is also the way I want to leave this life remembering these two young men who have found joy in the middle of life's messes!

That picture gives me cause to stand in faith for every member of our family—that their joy will be made full! The biggest reason that photograph stirs such faith in me is that it represents the power of God to heal and restore broken relationships. You see, there was a time when Grayson and Keaton were not the best of friends. They had some challenging issues in childhood—issues that could have forever separated them had not God been at work behind the scenes working in each of their lives and in the lives of their family.

BETTER NOT BITTER

When these two boys were very small, their parents divorced. As with any divorce, there is always heartbreak. And while there have been some very difficult roads to walk for each of them, I have seen God do amazing things in their lives. I offer their story with their permission so that you might find hope because what God has done for them is nothing short of miraculous.

As boys they shared similar struggles but with very different perspectives. With the divorce, one boy was swept unexpectedly into the role of cheering up his mom and being an ever-ready listening ear for her broken heart, and the other boy was swept into the role of finding his "rightful place as older brother" in a family that was no longer "normal." Normal, as they knew, was forever gone. They had to find a new normal.

Through years of ups and downs, high and lows, and some "dark places" as Keaton calls it, what they eventually discovered is "the very hardship of life with no normal and the sense of constant struggle to measure up to what the people in our environment demanded" became the stuff that could either make them bitter or better. Eventually, they arrived on "the other side of messy" as better men.

And yet, you might imagine that it took *more than they could have ever anticipated* in making them the good men that they are becoming. The shared experience of growing up as brothers in a broken home impacted their lives so differently because of their unique perspectives. Let me explain.

GRAYSON

Grayson has had the role of friend, confidant, son, and brother—all through his childhood, and adolescence. Even now as a young adult, he swears he made it through because God kept him oblivious to the seriousness of it all. Like a river that keeps on rolling—over rocks and stones, bends and waterfalls—Grayson just went with the flow because that is what he had to do.

His mom was sad, his brother was withdrawn, so Grayson just did what he had to do—get out of bed, make sure the others were up too, just kind of naturally take on the role of trying to keep everybody moving forward. But, in doing that, Grayson never learned to peer relate until high school—so friendships that most people have were just "not there". Now, he would tell you that he was socially incompetent, made complete with his unmistakable laugh. But it was not always fun or funny.

KEATON

Keaton, on the other hand, had been relentlessly bullied in grade school. So, he spent a good deal of time trying to find out how to fit in, how to make people notice him, how to make people like him. And, Keaton was searching for people who value him simply for who he is.

In the process of trying to figure out life and protect his heart, Keaton developed a somewhat sarcastic sense of humor that was not always appreciated by others (even though it now may keep his brother and most of us laughing for hours). Let's just say, there were plenty of times that he was misunderstood. In those "dark places", Keaton was deeply lonely. Bottom line: he struggled to find his own place, not because he was not loved by his mom or his dad—they love him dearly. It's just that divorce complicates things—stuff happens. It is just the way life can be.

In addition to all of this, Keaton is first in the birth order of his family. First birth order children tend to experience a significantly larger lifetime deposit of added expectations from their family. They rise to those expectations to the degree of support they receive especially from their parents in their formative years and from other adults who believe in them over the course of that lifetime.

The pressured often-unconscious demand of the environment makes the self-*confident* grow in responsibility and the self-*conscious* run for shelter. Keaton ran in search of his worth, all the while feeling overwhelmed by his life. He medicated his pain as safely as he knew how, but he was drowning internally with people all around him, some clinging to him. At a time when most people would have fallen totally apart, one day after great heartbreak, he decided to toss all fantasy aside that something or someone else was going to fix him.

Keaton chose to believe that God created him to live in Reality *from then on*—that God was the only one Who would give him power to be the man he was searching for: Keaton, the worthwhile active agent, the sole creative writer of his joy-full life story. He has "never been the same" since that day. And the story that will never be the same again continues!

JOY-GIVER NOT JOY-STEALER

The simple truth of the matter is that divorce is hard on everyone. And, as a result, children impacted by divorce tend to struggle with having fun because they feel the responsibility to perform to meet other people's expectations. Even young children, unconsciously or subconsciously, blame themselves for their parents' conflict and the breakup of their family.

So, they rarely have, find, or make time for spontaneous fun or time to deeply connect with others—they are "too busy carrying" this huge weight of responsibility. However, having watched all of this from the sidelines, this is what I have come to know and deeply treasure: *God uses the secret ingredient of heartbreak in all our lives to shape us. Our pain becomes one of the essential ingredients for our potential.*

Ultimately, what these two brothers share in common (their life story) has caused them to grow into each other's best allies. Today, they want good things for one another; they believe in one another's dreams; they will tell anyone who asks that they are each other's best friend. The outcome is that God is shaping these young men into the kind of brothers they have always wanted to be—Best Friends—full of the joy they once were missing, but now possess!

JUST DO WHATEVER HE SAYS

Here is a truth you may know—In our hard places and shattered shambles, we have no idea how to even *anticipate healing* before it comes to us. Our choices can contribute to it, but we cannot make it happen on demand. There is no checklist to tell us what it will take and no performance prize to reward us.

Do you also know this? Do you know that our willingness *to participate in our healing* and our willingness *to receive our healing* are more valuable than we can comprehend?

Understand this: When Jesus turned the water into wine, in John chapter two, he could have performed that miracle in several ways. He could have just said, "Let there be wine!" And there would have been wine. But that's not what He did. Instead, He chose to involve others in the work of His first miracle. "His mother [Mary] told the servants, 'Do whatever he tells you.'

... Jesus said to the servants, 'Fill the jars with water. And they filled them up to the brim."[17] They wholeheartedly participated— filling the jars all the way to the top!

PARTNERING WITH GOD

Here is what we see happening in the text that continues to be true in life NOW: God involves us as working participating partners in His work and we, just like they did, share in the blessing that comes from the results. They were the first to see a miracle. And this is a pattern of how He works in our lives too. We will see miracles when we partner with Him.

As God began to work in Grayson and Keaton's individual lives, inviting them to participate with Him in His work, they reaped the blessing of partnering with God. That is just what God does and always has done when people say "yes" to His invitation to partner with Him.

I cannot help but think that, when God invited me to participate with Him in the healing of my family—back when I first gathered my grandchildren for the "Santa Fe Summit", conversations began to happen that would have never happened otherwise. Over the course of years that have followed "The Summit," as Grayson and Keaton have grown into manhood, those open and honest conversations laid the foundation that eventually allowed them to see and understand each other's struggles in a new light. Those conversations paved the way for more conversations which in turn gave birth to compassion for one another and to becoming the best of friends. They could keep each other company for hours and they do!

JOY LOVES PARTNERSHIP

So, do you see it now? Our willingness to participate in our healing and our willingness to receive healing are more valuable than we could possibly know. When God invites us into His work and we participate in the work, we reap the joy of blessings. Without our participation, that photo that hangs on my wall, the one I love so much, might never have been taken. Thank God for His invitation to partner with Him! It has brought about much blessing in the lives of our family.

Nowadays, whenever I think back on those early years, when the heartbreak of my daughter's divorce was so fresh and the little lives of Keaton and Grayson were in turmoil, all I have to do is look at that photo that hangs on my wall.

In that photo, which captures the ecstatic joy of two brothers enjoying life to the full, is the reality of what I once hoped for, the proof of what I had not yet seen—that proof has now come full circle.

I can say beyond a shadow of doubt "with God all things are possible"! Yes, life can be full of joy—when we partner with God!

Keaton Leak & Grayson Leak

Defeat Generational Dysfunction, Find Generational Freedom
Three Empowering Principles with Three Equipping Questions to Fight FOR YOUR FAMILY

CHAPTER FIVE

Principle One. Joyful freedom is found beyond circumstantial happiness.

Scripture: James 1:2-3 (NIV) "Consider it pure joy, my brothers, whenever you face trials of many kinds, because you know that the testing of your faith develops perseverance."

Explanation: Happiness comes and goes because circumstances change. Joy increases with time because you understand that God is working His plan for your good every day, no matter what the circumstances are. Average people let their feelings lead them. Healthy successful people lead with the vision God has given them for their lives and maximize their relationships with one another. They know they cannot live the joyful life they desire without others who believe God.

Question 1.

Since perseverance leads to greater things God has promised, why are trials necessary and good?

Question 2.

Since faith is belief put into action, how do you plan to use your challenges more effectively?

Question 3.

One weight produces a level of strength, greater weight produces more strength. Does believing for more joy cause you to expect more testing? Why or why not?

Principle Two. Joy is possessable when you find it in partnership.

Scripture: Philippians 1:3-6 (NIV) "I thank my God every time I remember you. 4 In all my prayers for all of you, I always pray with joy because of your partnership in the gospel from the first day until now, 6 being confident of this, that He Who began a good work in you will carry it on to completion until the day of Christ Jesus."

Explanation: Great people go through the greatest challenges—Paul was no exception. Without doubt, his partners made a significant difference—present or from a distance. He remembered life was not all about him. He wisely began to focus on the difference they made in one another's lives. He believed for himself and for them that God was faithfully growing them into the people who would be able to receive all He created for them to enjoy. Their shared joy was multiplied.

Question 1.

What have you lost by only focusing on yourself and the efforts of your personal achievements?

Question 2.

How much more has been produced by partnership, and what joy has it produced despite obstacles?

Question 3.

How will you *possess and increase your joy* through investing in partnerships going forward?

Principle Three. Joy is sharable beyond partnership because results multiply.

Scripture: Philippians 2:2-4 (NIV) "...make my joy complete by being like-minded, having the same love, being one in spirit and purpose. 3 Do nothing out of selfish ambition or vain conceit, but in humility consider others better than yourselves. 4 Each of you should look not only to your own interests, but also to the interests of others."

Explanation: Research tells us that people get more joy from giving than from receiving. God designed life to be that way. Whatever we do together produces sharable joy. What we produce together multiplies the joy for others—we cannot contain its effect. Humility is a supernatural result of recognizing the valuable role each person plays. Joy creates a better future every day. It exceeds limits caused by past or present circumstances. Joy does not run out, it multiplies.

Question 1.

How have past circumstances limited your enjoyment, because you let everything depend on you?

Question 2.

What are you willing to rethink and reconsider to partner with God and others to multiply joy?

Question 3.

How will you re-assess your resources, recognize what you and others bring to the table, and partner more effectively with God to bless the lives of more people than ever before?

Chapter Six
LAUGH AGAIN: LET GO AND LET GOD

JUST A CONVERSATION

My husband Mike's birthday was just around the corner. Plans had been swirling in my head for weeks about making this birthday "his best birthday ever".

My niece and I were talking about the party plans when our conversation drifted to memories of past family gatherings. I said to Meredith, "You know, I can remember the best Thanksgiving I ever had."

We had been talking about how I love to *do* Thanksgiving in our home because there are so many people who have no place to go. If I did not *do* thanksgiving they would not be invited anywhere. I could hardly stand the thought of that. Truly, that is one of the two reasons I love to *do* Thanksgiving. The other reason is simply the joy of having the whole family gathered around our table.

But nowadays, after the kids' divorces, everyone is potentially displaced. One says, "I have to take the kids there," another says, "I have to take the boys here," and the nieces and nephews have to be over there. Everybody *could* be elsewhere. Our Thanksgivings have become a little smaller. Even the thought of it makes me sad.

I SAID IT AND I'M STICKIN' TO IT!

So, Meredith said, "Well, tell me about your best Thanksgiving ever. When was it, Francie?" Without delay I answered, "It was when Mike and I were separated, and my brother and his wife Carolyn invited me over to their home. And, of course, I went." The look on Meredith's face begged for clarification.

"So, I loaded my dogs into my truck and drove fifty miles to Conroe—just me and the dogs and the little bit of stuff that I had cooked—a tiny offering compared to the love and shelter my brother offered me on that cold brisk beautiful Thanksgiving Day. When I arrived, they were deep frying turkeys in the garage. Mother was already there. I walked into the house and everything was ready, the table handsomely set, and for the first time ever I quietly said to myself, 'Wow! I am coming as a guest!'"

I explained, "Meredith, for as long as can remember I have loved the Disney song, 'Be Our Guest' from 'Beauty and the Beast.' I think the song is magnificent! I love every word of it because it truly does explain in that song how you always want to feel as a guest. And then of course, you always want your guests to feel as though they are being treated like that song."

"So, at the end of the day, I loaded up the dogs and headed back to Houston. I will never forget what I was thinking on the quiet drive home: 'Wow, just wow! This day was *exceptionally* relaxing! I went to somebody else's home and enjoyed a beautiful Thanksgiving dinner that I did not have to worry about three days prior. And, and I am NOT going to be cleaning up until midnight? What a fantastic day!'"

SURPRISE

I am pretty sure Meredith had *never* heard me say anything like that, because I am *never* the guest—I am always the hostess. It is *my thing*, and everybody knows it! So, imagine my surprise when Meredith looked at me and said, "Well Mia, so glad you shared this story, because this time, I want to cook the birthday dinner for Uncle Mike! For twenty-five years, you have cooked every dinner, thrown every party, and hosted every holiday affair. You have done it all and we have loved it! But you have *never* once let us help. Let me do this, please!"

I have to say; Meredith had never been so bold. The truth of the matter is—it made me *feel bad.* And even though I kind of knew she was *right*—that it was time for me to step back and let others have an opportunity to serve—I hurriedly countered, "Well, you *never* asked me. You have *never* once said, 'Can I come over and cook the dinner?'" You always just said, "Can I bring something?" And I have always said, "Yes, bring your brownies."

LET THERE BE LIGHT

Now, maybe it was just coincidence (but I do not think so) that she would ask to cook Mike's birthday dinner when lately I have been thinking about so many things—urgent things and pressing matters, things stirring in my soul. Things I am sure one only thinks about in the winter of one's life. It has not escaped me, that I am seventy. I may live for five more years or I may only live for five more minutes. So, in my spirit there has been an increasing sense of urgency. I am constantly thinking, whether I'm taking a shower or taking a walk, whether I am cooking or cleaning—these are thoughts that creep into my mind: "Have I shared enough? Have I loved enough? Have I given enough? Have I done enough for my family?"

So, when Meredith asked if she could cook the meal, I felt like God said, "Let her do this. It is time for you to let others shine in the things that you have taught them. Step back."

Without hesitation, I said, "Have at it, girl! You may cook the meal!" I let her do the whole party and the room looked stunning. She let the children and Grayson, who was visiting, decorate. My niece and nephews (Sofia, Drake, Alex, and Santiago) beamed with excitement to be a part of making the room so beautiful. There were balloons and confetti everywhere, a beautiful cake and a table magnificently set for the four-course meal she prepared. It was a night to remember—a birthday celebration that neither Mike nor I will ever forget! It was spectacular in every way: an evening filled with laughter and love!

BEFORE AND AFTER

Without a doubt, I believe the evening's joy was multiplied because I stepped back and let others come forward; because, it is time for them to shine. I am beginning to understand more completely that, when God led me four plus years ago to invite the grandchildren to my Santa Fe home for what we have now lovingly dubbed "the Santa Fe Summit," certain things were set in motion. Those "Battle Board" strategy sessions (where we agreed to talk openly, honestly, and without judgment about behaviors that had impacted each of their lives) are beginning to bear fruit—much fruit.

We are setting family benchmarks in place in this chapter by saying that Brooke is now living in California discovering many new possibilities for herself. Alli has graduated college and beginning a business marketing career in real estate. Both Keaton and Grayson have a strong footing in their respective colleges—searching for meaningful work that will cause them to soar. Ciera and Brittany just started first semesters in their colleges and are discovering amazing things they never knew about themselves.

In fact, it has been like viewing a set of *"Before" and "After" pictures* because there has been such significant progress in each of their lives. Quite simply, I had no idea that the process God led me into would be so deep and so far-reaching when I invited my grandkids to gather around our table of love and just "tell the truth".

I WILL NEVER BE THE SAME AGAIN

Furthermore, I had no idea how transforming it would be for me in a very personal way—I am seeing our lives in a very different way now. The transformation is becoming increasingly obvious. When I pause long enough to look back, I find myself pondering the reality of just how deeply and just how far God has brought us in what really is a very short time!

There have been a lot of changes over the last four and half years or so; some major shifts and transitions. They have not all been easy. There have been some days that I have had to consider the reality that I cannot be everything for everybody as much as I would love to be.

When my daughter recently moved away, it was the first time we have been apart in fifty years! So, you can imagine, it has been a bit overwhelming. Hard as that was, it was not as much about letting Tammy go. I knew the move would be good for Tammy. The issue that bothered me the most and that worried my heart sick was the fact that my grandsons would no longer have a place to call home or a mom to greet them at their front door with hugs and kisses when they were back in Houston for holidays and summer breaks. I did not want them to *ever* feel lost and without a sense of belonging.

But, speaking of progression and embracing change, these boys are thriving despite my worrying heart. Over this past summer break, we shared several meals together. We talked about Keaton's great apartment and he chimed in, "Yeah Mia, the apartment's great and my suite-mates are great! When I'm not studying, we really have a good time. I enjoy being there. I enjoy the campus. Truth, Mia: for the first time ever—I actually love going to all my classes." He was so happy.

Then Grayson grinned at me like only he can and said, "Mia, I love Santa Fe; it is where we spend our summers; it's my favorite place in the whole world. But I cannot wait to get back to Samford! I'm going to be the president of a club this year!" And I said, "My goodness, look at the two of you and all that you have already!"

FROM OVERWHELM TO PURE DELIGHT

And there it was— peace—in the middle of my worry. From overwhelm to pure delight, gone was the weight of worry. When their summer ended and those two boys, and Ciera & Brittany packed their bags and walked out my front door, I had nothing but peace. Because, everything was as it should be. Everything was okay. Then, I said to myself, "Francie, you are not going to worry about this anymore. You are going to have fun. Just like the chapter title says, *Seriously Choosing to Laugh Again.* And I am having fun— so much fun! Just thinking about those boys and my granddaughters and their enthusiasm for this season in their lives ... makes my heart full of joy.

Come to think of it, there has been a steady flow of "before" and "after" pictures which I am only just now beginning to connect. God has granted me the joy and privilege of watching my grandchildren being transformed into the people He has created them to be. I think it has something to do with the fact that I said "Yes" to God all those years ago.

Oh, to be sure, there is still much for God to do in their precious lives. But they are embracing life with all its challenges just like we talked about years ago. I now have the pleasure of stepping back to watch those "battle board" strategies come to fruition.

CIERA: FINDING COURAGE

Only months ago, I chatted with Ciera while she was packing for her trip to Africa. All kinds of stuff were strewn all over the room as she frantically tried to cram as much of her life as possible into that one suitcase. If you had not known better, you would have thought she was never coming back. She picked up a large photo album: a year's worth of senior photos that cost us an arm and leg, ones she swore up and down that she had to have because it would be her "forever treasure"! I tried to tell her, "Darlin', after this year is over, you will probably never look at those photos again (maybe once in a blue moon)." She said what you would expect her to say, "No way! I will take these photos wherever I go in life. I promise." So dramatic—but so effective—O yes, we capitulated. We bought the years' worth of pictures. Oh, the endless joys of grandparenting!

However, on that summer day, as Ciera stood in the middle of a pile of clothes while clutching the "treasured" photo album to her chest, she looked at me and murmured, "Mia, you were so right, who I was in these pictures is not who I am becoming. Everything that is important lies in front of me, not behind me. I get it now, Mia." And just like that, she chucked that photo album into a pile of stuff labeled "non-essential."

With the closing zip of her suitcase, the girl was gone, and a young woman stood before me—only I did not know it at the time. We rarely do. I do not think she knew it either. We do not usually recognize the transformation moment—we do not usually see it—until we can look at the "before" and "after" pictures—the old and new, laid side by side, and it takes our breath away! We marvel to ourselves and wonder, "Where did the little girl go, the one so often overwhelmed that she could barely find her voice, the one who second guessed every decision she ever made, the one scared to make a move because she was certain she would mess it up or do it wrong." And, when did this beautiful expression of a woman emerge whose smile could light up a village on the other side of our globe?

SOWING TEARS AND REAPING JOY

Ciera found her courage when she boarded that plane, even though I knew she was scared she would do this trip all wrong (like so many of her passing worries) and afraid she would never be good enough to make a significant contribution in the lives of those children living there. Well, she impacted their lives for sure, but they surely equally impacted her life as well. She walked the ramp to the door of that plane with a heart full of fear and insecurities. She returned home with a heart confident in the goodness of God to use her gifts with her imperfections for His glory and for the good of people she had never known before.

With sundrenched skin, she beamed with joy and laughter as she told of her adventure half way around the world. She said, "I struggled the first few days because I felt like *my story paled in comparison to the sadness and sorrow these children had endured.* Their lives were so different from mine. Many of them were orphans with no parent to love them when they got sick or put new shoes on their feet when the ones they were wearing fell to pieces. I saw suffering and hardships like I have never seen before. And so, I could not imagine how I could possibly bring anything of value to their situation."

She went on, "Then I remembered, it was not about me. Even though I did not think I was worthy to be there, I knew that I had come to make a difference, I needed to stand strong, and I needed to give those children my love and my friendship. As I opened up and shared parts of my own story with others, those people became like family. We shared dinners and talked long into the night. I met a lot of really good people. It was amazing what happened once I opened up and gave away my heart. Before the week was done, I had kids holding onto me all the time. I can still see their beautiful faces beaming with bright happy smiles."

She grew introspective; spoke in almost a whisper when she said, "I started to see that life is so much more than all the little things we so easily take for granted in America. One sweet little girl's shoes had broken, the soles had fallen completely apart, and she cried so hard. It just broke my heart because I did not know what to do. In America, in my life, this is so foreign to me. We never give it a moment's thought. We do not worry about not having shoes for feet. If our shoes break, we just go buy a new pair. Our normal is not found in Africa in the village of Bungoma, where so many children have so very little. Yet, I have rarely seen or ever been part of such joy."

Wrapping up her story she said, "I gave away every pair of shoes I brought with me, except for the pair I was wearing, and nothing has ever felt so good. The only regret I had was that it took me two or three days to really nestle in and love those children—I wish I would have done it sooner because it would have allowed for even more changes to take place. And leaving... well, that was just horrible, heart-rending. Every one of my teammates bawled like babies—we just so connected with those children. It felt different than any other mission trip I have ever been on. Lots of tears. But, so worth it! And, I can't wait to go back."

A FRONT ROW SEAT

Gosh, I wish you could what I see now. There's a beautiful "After" photo of "Ciera, the Courageous" that sits on my bedside table. Truthfully, the photo looks like it belongs on the cover of Life Magazine. In the photo, my Ciera is walking down a long dusty road in Africa. Her face is beaming in the light of the Kenyan sun and she is surrounded by a dozen or more beautiful Bungoma children. I have never seen her look so complete and so full of confident joy!

Oh, how this journey of simply inviting my grandchildren to talk openly and honestly without shame or judgment has changed all our lives, including mine. I did not know when I invited the grandchildren all those years ago to "identify their biggest obstacles" for "the purpose of finding strategies to overcome future challenges" that I would be granted a front row seat to the handiwork of God revealed in and through their lives. I did not know I would be seeing beautiful "before and after" pictures of each of them, but I have! I have had the joy of watching them move from overwhelm to delight as they have embraced their challenges head-on.

And, if I could encourage you in one thing, this is what I would say, "Get *your own* front row seat. Create your own haven of peace— a safe place for your children and grandchildren to *tell the truth in love* without fear of shame or blame. Meet them where they are and let God do the rest. You will never regret the conversations you will share around the table of love.

I also did not recognize a kind of impact I have made to my family's *way of being family.* You see, I do take things more seriously than I thought I did, and I do take responsibility more than I should. All along, my family has been watching. And we—*we are seriously learning to laugh...again!* And I have got good news for you...you can too!

Mike Sophia Drake Santiago Alex

Meredith De Olavarria Sophia Marchione

Ciera Willis with her African Students

Defeating Generational Dysfunction, Finding Generational Freedom

Three Empowering Principles with Three Equipping Questions to Fight FOR YOUR FAMILY

CHAPTER SIX

Principle One. We can laugh because God in us makes us enough.

Scripture: 2 Corinthians 12:9-10 (NIV) "But [God] said to me, 'My grace is sufficient for you, for My power is made perfect in weakness.' Therefore, I will boast all the more gladly about my weaknesses, so that Christ's power may rest on me. That is why, for Christ's sake, I delight in weaknesses, in insults, in hardships, in persecutions, in difficulties. For when I am weak, then I am strong."

Explanation: When is "enough enough" for us or for others? Perhaps, this is a rhetorical question. God takes that question seriously; encouraging us to lighten up. He tells us that, where we are weak or lacking, He completes us. He empowers us to do our part and does His part with His power. Delighting in our weaknesses sounds strange, but this verse is better understood by saying "I choose to think well of myself no matter what because God is strong enough for both of us.

Question 1.

Where are you likely to need God most in your day, in your work, in your relationships?

Question 2.

Who is more likely to think little of you when you lack, others or you? What would you expect God's response would be to that?

Question 3.

Why do people struggle with laughing at themselves? What would make it easier for you to be able to see the humor in what you do or find challenging? Where is the genuine smile in this?

Principle Two. We can laugh because God controls all our tomorrows.

Scripture: 1 Peter 5:7 (NIV) "Cast all your anxiety on Him because He cares for you."

Explanation: In this verse, "anxiety" is stressing ahead of time about something real or imagined that you doubt you can handle. We are told to hurl our anxiety like a hot potato into God's hands because He cares enough to control for us what we cannot that is up ahead of us. If God knows already and is prepared, it is somewhat hilarious that we are stressed that we might have to back Him up in case He needs our help. Choose to be at ease, and a smile might appear!

Question 1.

How long has it been since you have laughed at yourself because you got yourself all tied up about what turned out to be nothing? If you can laugh, it will be because this has happened enough that this is not your first time.

Question 2.

What is the hot potato that you hold onto far too long and far too frequently? What would make you release more quickly, even smile when you realize you need to release the stress?

Question 3.

Who could help you get a handle on getting serious about letting go and letting God?

Principle Three. We can laugh because God is working in us until perfection.

Scripture: Philippians 1:3-6 (MSG) "Every time you cross my mind, I break out in exclamations of thanks to God. 4 Each exclamation is a trigger to prayer. I find myself praying for you with a glad heart. 5 I am so pleased that you have continued in this with us, believing and proclaiming God's Message, from the day you heard it right up to the present. 6 There has never been the slightest doubt in my mind that the God who started this great work in you would keep at it and bring it to a flourishing finish on the very day Christ Jesus appears."

Explanation: You are not in this alone unless you believe you are and choose to be. God considers Himself to be your Partner in this life and has prepared others to join in your journey. He will complete all that He has planned for you. He has perfectly designed you for a mission that is not to be completed alone. You must admit, if you survive alone or thrive alone, you would be the only person in history to do that. It is time to laugh, improve the results, and enjoy the ride.

Question 1.

Paul was so grateful to discover that using his willpower to perform up to his standards was not what God desired. How have your standards and use of your willpower effected your life?

Question 2.

Who will you have to ask for help OR who will you ask to help... to ease the load and get happy?

Question 3.

What is the next step for you to begin to let God be Himself and let you be yourself?

Chapter Seven
ENCOURAGE HEALTHY RELATIONSHIPS

In a recent conversation with a new friend, I heard words which I had never heard before. He said, *"Living in a state consumed by driven-ness is considered unhealthy; it is called 'dis-ease'."* Disease? I had never thought about that. But, coming to think about it now "made new sense". There is nothing easy about driven ness.

Then he asked this question: "If being 'overwhelmed' is not bad in and of itself, what do you find that you have been 'overwhelmed by' that has also 'driven you?'"

NOT ROCKET SCIENCE

It did not take but a few seconds for the answer to come to me, and yet my answer surprised me. It surprised me in that it just rolled off my tongue so quickly unguarded and without reservation. And I, I was unashamed to own it because...it was true. Even if I had never admitted to anyone else, it was true. And it just came flying out of my mouth: "Fear, mostly fear. In my life, it has been fear." Not for myself, ever, however, fear for my family.

Yes, that's what I said—and it was the truth. I have been fearful for my whole life—*fearful for all my family*—my parents, my brother Gary, my nephew Ty, my nieces Meredith, Lisa, and Kelley, my husband Mike, my children (Tammy, Mike Jr, Mark, Deborah, and Avery), fearful for my grandchildren (Brooke, Alli, Jake, Brittany,

Ciera, Trevor, Grayson and Keaton), fearful for my great niece and great nephews (Sophia, Drake, Santiago, Alejandro, William, and Finn), and *fearful in every overwhelming situation*. In fact, I have been fear-driven *until some years ago!*

I have to say this again: This process of inviting my grandchildren to share in open, honest, non-judgmental conversations about their obstacles and challenges *has profoundly impacted my life*. In fact, I do not know that I would have ever told anyone, let alone every reader of this book, that I, Francie Willis, have spent a good deal of my life being driven by fear. This process of sharing deep conversations with the grandchildren and the writing of this book has brought greater clarity in my own life—my own soul—and I am better for it.

I AM NOT ALONE

Truthfully, I think it is part of human nature to be fear driven. Being fear-driven started all the way back in the garden of Eden with the fall of man and our severed relationship with God. However, Jesus came to restore all that was lost in the fall.

So, because I belong to Him, I tell myself often (as I told my Mother every day the last year of her life): "Jesus told not us to worry. Why are we worrying? What can we do about worry?" I have thought long and hard about this, and two facts have become a big deal to me for quite a few years now: (A) The very clear fact that we are told "Do not worry", and (B) The very clear fact that "We gain nothing through fear." This is going somewhere—so stay with me—because, this could be as eye-opening for you as it has been for me.

OVERWHELMED

Speaking from the heart, I must tell you that I have been overwhelmed for my whole life long. Only now, *I am learning that there are better ways to be overwhelmed.* I am learning that being a "human doing" (a person overwhelmed with doing) is not what I was created to be. I have been created for so much more and so have you. So, are you ready to hear what I have been learning?

First, I have come to realize that *the world does not fall apart* when I stop doing. Oh yes, it will go on!

Second, I have come to grips with the fact that *I can choose* to love being overwhelmed *with joy.*

Third, I love *being overwhelmed*—if you want to know the truth.

I have chaired every event there was to chair in our city. And yes, each one seemed to be like having a baby—it took nine months and intense labor to pull it off and, in the end, you are totally *overwhelmed.* But what great fulfillment we experienced when needs were met, and lives were transformed! So, when I think about being overwhelmed, I always go back to that. Having the satisfaction of meeting deadline after deadline in my philanthropy and work, driving one project after the next, checking off every seasonal celebration in anticipation of another—I loved being overwhelmed with all of it!

When I owned Urban Retreat Day Spa and Salon, for well over two decades, every Christmas Season at Urban Retreat was spectacular. It was intense, but full of joy, because we always looked forward to selling hundreds of thousands of gift certificates *which was The Triple Win*—great for our staff, great for our guests, and great for our company! Every one of our staff members looked forward to the coming year and the wonderful guests that we would have the privilege of serving. That hard work, those long hours—now that was a good overwhelm and one that culminated in a lifetime of friendships.

HUMAN BEING

So, what is *"The Difference"*? What makes one thing healthy and another thing unhealthy? Underneath it all, I KNOW that I AM a human BEING and that YOU are a human BEING. While *the Overwhelm of the task* at hand is flowing, we get caught up in the self-conscious state of *what* do we have to *do* next and who is *doing it* with us. We have the enormous satisfaction of a job well-done and the shared fun that goes with it. But typically, we are more conscious of ourselves during it than we are intentional about building our relationships with quality interaction. More times than we would probably care to admit, the intentionality of relationship building goes by the wayside because we are too task-focused and not enough relationship-focused.

For example, do people KNOW that I AM a human BEING? Do people know that it is *my deep desire* for them to know how *important and special they are to me*? Do they all know that I really care about them? I often think about those who have worked *for me and with me* and I wonder "Did they know how much they meant to me? Like Armando, did he know that he was so much more than just the valet attendant? Did he know that in every kind of weather, be it the sweltering heat of a summer day, or a cold wet winter rain, he set the bar on what faithfulness in the workplace looked like? I never once remember him complaining—I just remember the smile on his face as he served with the utmost of integrity.

And oh my, the faces that come to mind when I think of all the individuals who made those days at Urban Retreat the sweetest days ever. I think of Mario, faithful grounds keeper and facility maintenance manager who kept everything in impeccable order, and then there are the housekeepers, shampoo technicians, appointment coordinators, front desk and administrative staff, the boutique manager, and of course the most talented team of service providers one could ever hope to have. Oh, I hope with all my heart they know how precious they were and still are to me.

Therefore, I cannot help but wonder, *Do the people that we love most know* that they are not simply a *"means to an end"? Do they see through the demanding rush of busyness that they mean the world to us?*

PEOPLE MATTER MOST

Writing this book in 2018 & 2019 has certainly caused me to think deeply about what matters most—the people I hold dear and precious to my heart. I want to be sure that my relationships are healthy and that my thoughts translate into an attitude that produces words and actions that truly build the people I sometimes forget that I influence—the people I cross paths with every day of my life!

But, especially our grandchildren, niece and nephews ...

Just a couple of months ago, several of the grandchildren were vacationing together on a cruise to the Bahamas. The "after" stories, from the adventure they shared, have been delightful and remarkably insightful. Oh my, can I just say, "they are becoming highly aware of the impact they have upon each other."

I never knew how much joy could come from watching my kids or grandkids, niece, and nephews discover as adults that *the relationships they share with others become easy when they freely give and receive encouragement.*

For example, I have one grandchild that is *germophobic* and the thought of public places (like shared bathrooms and locker rooms) drive her crazy! Ciera will tell you straight up, "That's me!" She is my agenda-driven darling who finds it hard to let go and just have fun. Although, you would never know that from her photos–she is all smiles like a happy-go-lucky kind of girl. She can put on a good face when she needs to, but deep down inside, sometimes she must push herself to hang out with people, especially if it is at a waterpark! And that's exactly where Ciera found herself on the cruise. Thank goodness for Alli whose encouragement made all the difference in the world!

Ciera said, "I was so uptight, like I always am. I do not like water parks. Everyone knows that. I think they are dirty, disgusting, and just nasty—Germs everywhere! I do not even want to get in the water— especially the Lazy River—yuck—that is just the grossest! But here we were at Atlantis and all the siblings and cousins wanted to go down the water slides. So, I was like 'Okay, guess we are going down the slides—NOT I!' Everyone else was going to enjoy the slides, but not me. Nope, I was just following along because *that is what I do.* On the way to the waterslides, we stopped by the restrooms and I was like 'Hmmm, let me grab my shoes first—those floors are dirty.' But Alli, who doesn't ever wear shoes at a waterpark, was like, 'Oh my gosh! Live a little!' Yep, it was grin and bear it time! So, I was like 'Yay! This is going to be so much fun!' But I was lying through my teeth! I did not want to be there at all!

LIVE A LITTLE

But I must tell you, after I went down that slide, I glanced back at Alli. Our eyes locked. And I, I hollered out 'Oh my gosh that was so freaking fun!' I am telling you it was *so fun*. I felt free—I let loose—and had a blast! Thank God Alli pushed me to *'live a little!'* Best vacation ever!"

That shared vacation brought about keen insights too from some of the other siblings as well.

As with any trip when families are packed together for days on end, sometimes tensions can run a little high. It is just life and trying to keep everybody happy is not always easy, because well, we are all so different.

But, once we get that and we start to appreciate others for who they really are, it becomes so much easier to focus on the relationship rather than the differences. It is a funny thing, but when we take our eyes off of ourselves, we actually begin to move from self-consciousness to relationship-consciousness and we become intentional about quality interaction. Yes indeed, *live a little!*

UNEXPECTED BEAUTIFUL MOMENTS

Brooke and Alli, as sisters, had their own "Aha!" moments. It was kind of beautiful. Brooke, the oldest grandchild, has always been a free spirit. She said, "We are at this point in life where we need to just let everyone be themselves. Because, at this point, we all know who the other person is—at least we think we do. And to "recognize that" is to create less stress when we all come together. If we would be empathic and sympathetic with "who we all are", then there will never be cause for much tension between all of us and our differences." She is growing wise and I love that viewpoint.

Alli came to a very similar conclusion. She said, "My siblings and I are now older, and we are finally forming into "our individual humans". We are learning that we are not always going to get along or agree on how life should be lived. Brooke is more free-spirited, goofy, and silly too. Jake is more reserved and quieter—that does not mean he is rude, or he does not want to hang out with the family. It's just who he is. And we are all noticing these differences now that we are older."

She continued, "So we are learning to respect each other's own personalities—because even though we are siblings, we are not at all the same. We are learning to respect each other so that we do not fight and overstep our boundaries when we are talking with each other. So yeah, we are learning to see each other not as "our flaws", but as those things which make each of us unique." My goodness, what wisdom! They are learning to be intentional with one another—to encourage each other just as they are!

Had my grandchildren been unwilling to enter this magnificent conversation with me, I might never have experienced the conversations I have shared with God over the course of writing this book with and for my grandchildren, niece, and nephews.

Sitting here, writing these words, I cannot help but be grateful that God found a way to slow me down long enough to break me out of the performance trap and into becoming the wife, mother, and grandmother that I need to be right now—in this moment. Because, currently in my life I am "feeling the seasons" down deep in my bones, I am acutely aware of the importance of *these days.*

BEING AND DOING BEGINS WITH GOD

In this season, I am finding that God can show me things that I have never seen before. More fully than ever, I believe He wants conversation with me; wants to spend time with me rather than just give me a download of information. You need to know that God is not interested in giving you a download, even from the Bible. He wants so much more for us than to be life information experts. He wants to reveal His unlimited life to us through an ever-deepening relationship with Him—right up to the moment we draw our last breath!

What I am discovering is that Jesus was not focused on solely meeting the needs of people, but rather focused first on BEING with His Father. When He first focused on being with His Father, DOING what His Father was "doing and showing" Him to do became His way of life. Time spent being with His Father was the prerequisite before any doing.

I admit that I have lacked in this area of BEING with the Father. In all honesty, the overwhelm that I have loved so much has stolen time that could have been better spent in intimacy with my Father. I am sure that I am not alone in this. I am certain that you understand.

I have the best of intentions. The alarm clock set for an early morning hour, long before the rest of my household stirs. But, as soon as my feet hit the floor, a million and one tasks compete for my attention. I think to myself; I must do this. I have to do that." And, if I do not wake up and have that special time with God—well then, I will talk to Him throughout the day and He will listen, but it's not the same. At the end of the day, I find myself apologizing for not giving Him the time He alone deserves.

Thankfully, God has not given up on me after all these years. He keeps ENCOURAGING my heart to focus more on the BEING and to let my DOING be a natural outcome of time spent with Him.

Ciera Alli & Brooke

Defeating Generational Dysfunction, Finding Generational Freedom
Three Empowering Principles with Three Equipping Questions to Fight FOR YOUR FAMILY

CHAPTER SEVEN

Principle One. We become encouraging when we serve "our" interests.

Scripture: Philippians 2:1-4 (NIV) "If you have any encouragement from being united with Christ, if any comfort from his love, if any fellowship with the Spirit, if any tenderness and compassion, 2 then make my joy complete by being like-minded, having the same love, being one in spirit and purpose. 3 Do nothing out of selfish ambition or vain conceit, but in humility consider others better than yourselves. 4 Each of you should look not only to your own interests, but also to the interests of others."

Explanation: Many people, believe it or not, struggle with encouragement because they are so focused on current circumstances or conditions. It is only really when we lift our eyes to look around us that we can see what could, should, and would be done better. Perseverance without encouragement is like sawing with a dull blade. Encouragement becomes more powerful when it grows from words to lending a hand. Encouragement comes from a changed mind and heart.

Question 1.

Who could you encourage? What words would make a daily difference that would express hope and your willingness to do things in a new way?

Question 2.

Who is likely to know who you could help or how you should help? When will you ask?

Question 3.

How can motives become shared to make improve our results? Consider shared thinking, love, spirit, and purpose...

Principle Two. We can become overwhelmed by love instead of fear.

Scripture: 1 John 4:18 (NIV)

"There is no fear in love. But perfect love drives out fear, because fear has to do with punishment. The one who fears is not made perfect in love."

Explanation: The Truth is that love—*action that communicates lasting commitment to relationship*—is delightfully overwhelming. One good reason is that there is no reason to be afraid of a relationship like that. God's love for us moves us from see *partially* to see *potential* to see *completion* in each other. Sometimes we need to be there for each other and at other times we need to do for each other. Sometimes we just need to be with each other. Fear is overpowered.

Question 1.

What fears do you see present in yourself? Where does your overwhelm live?

Question 2.

Where is real love present in your life? What relationships reveal lasting commitment?

Question 3.

What will you do today that will say to God "I want to be overwhelmed with Your love"?

Principle Three. We grow stronger as family by building each other up.

Scripture: 1 Thessalonians 5:11 (NIV) "...encourage one another and build each other up, just as in fact you are doing."

Explanation: There is never a bad time to practice building up someone you love. Simply giving your time to be present is a great start. Prioritizing each other speaks. When you prioritize your time alone with God it shows up in every other relationship. Doing is better done *together*, when doing *alone* for someone is not enough. Encouragement is a two-way street. God is just as willing to be with us as He is to do through us. Encouragement is a way to know His presence and power.

Question 1.

God never runs out of ideas. Ask Him to reveal new ways to build people you love. Ask Him to start with you.

Question 2.

Why is your encouragement needed? How does your presence make a difference?

Question 3.

What does it mean to you when someone you love is willing to speak and act for your good? What does it show that you need to see? How do you expect and want to reciprocate?

Generations

John T Willis & Mary Lambert Willis

Baker:
Morris, Norris, JP, Howard,
Anita, Stacey, James, and Charlie

Marchione:
Pete, Frank, Louie, Larry,
Pancrazio and Rose
Not pictured; Palma & Mary

Kyle, Grayson, Keaton, and Tammy Tyner Leak

Dawn, Mark, Alli, Brooke and Jake Willis

Mike, Lyndalin, Ciera, Trevor and Brittany Willis

Ty & Gary

Ty & Drake 2019

Chapter Eight
REGAIN POWER BY RELEASING CONTROL

There are those rare and beautiful moments in life where everything becomes unmistakably clear. Suddenly, you see connections once hidden with great clarity—how God was always with you—present in every high and every low, even when you could not see Him. He was ever near, never far, always there.

It is so similar to what happens when, as a novice hiker, you have climbed into the high country of the mountains and you are surprised that clouds have literally descended upon you—clouds so thick that you cannot see well enough to even place one foot in front of the other with confidence. Zero viability—nothing but clouds.

Then, an unanticipated wind suddenly begins to blow upon the mountain path beneath your feet. In what seems like moments, clouds are swept away and once again you can see everything as far as your eyes will take you. Glorious snowcapped mountains, flower-strewn valleys of green below wedged between rocks and lined by rivers have been there all the time—they were hidden from you before concealing clouds were rolled away.

I HAD A MOMENT

I had a moment just like that the other day when I stumbled upon a quote by N.T. Wright. Like one of those unanticipated reassuring winds, it blew through my mind and swept away a swirl of thick clouds that had kept me from truly seeing that I have never been without the presence of Jesus surrounding me. Rocky terrain and hard times have come and gone. He has come and never gone. I have never been alone. Gently revealed by Him, I now could see it all.

N. T. Wright declares with a sense of certainty what we often long for in our insecurity: "Those who go in Jesus' name, who get on with whatever work He gives them to do in His spirit and in His love are given an extraordinary status and privilege ... and *as you look back* you may be startled by the joy of realizing that as you walked in to that house, that hospital, that place of pain or love or sorrow or hope, Jesus was walking in wearing your skin, speaking in your voice."[18]

Do not miss the depth of what appears common: *as you look back*. Times come when each of us must *look back*. When we do, we are startled by the realization that, wherever we walked, Jesus entered wearing our skin and spoke through our voices. Still, we find ourselves speechless with wonder and joy.

Let that sink in as I did. You will see clouds part as His Holy Spirit uncovers the unseen and pours in the wisdom which reveals all the times that He clearly was moving in and through you. And you, yes you, will realize that you were just as unmistakably unaware as I was.

Those were the unlikeliest days—the days you felt so low it seemed your whole world was falling apart, yet you still loved in Jesus' name—in the name of that same Jesus Who said to His disciples "I will not leave you orphans; I will come to you."[19]

Oh yes, it is in *the looking back* that we are startled by joy because we can see that He did come to us!

In every hard, heartbreaking place, Jesus comes to us to encourage us to let go in a healthy way and to release to Him everything beyond our control which threatens to undo us. It is His gentle understanding way. When we find it uncomfortable to *let go and let God,* He is there even to help us release each and everything into the safety, security, and stability of His hands. As a woman, wife, mother, aunt, and grandmother, I can tell you that the hardest places of letting go and letting God concern issues regarding the people I love the most—my family.

Walk with me, think with me, stay with me through this chapter. There is a hope to be found for each of us and all of us.

HEARTBREAKING HISTORY

There is one unforgettable story in the history of America that I personally cannot read without weeping because it always touches my heart so close to home. I offer this story, as heart-rending as it may be, because I can tell you in the looking back I see that *He is the God Who "will not leave [us] as orphans"*[20] and does come to us in our time of need *when we place all that we love into the safekeeping of His hands.* [The following is a paraphrased account of The Orphan Train Movement[21]]

From the 1800's to the early 1900's, there was a significant inflow of immigrants who became United States citizens. These were men and women who came to America with hearts full of dreams and desires for better living. Foreigners with great ambitions to be landowners and business proprietors followed their dreams across the sea, just as my grandfather and grandmother did in

1914. America's eastern seaboard cities began to swell with tens of thousands of foreign-born entrepreneurs who spoke little to no English. Hope was their only currency.

Earning a living to provide for their families was much more difficult than they ever anticipated. Seriously hard times fell upon these families which caused many parents to eventually abandon their children because of their inability to care for them. Orphanages were created to provide for as many children as possible. But, many more of these young ones ended up living on the streets and became troublesome to those enforcing the laws.

In 1850, when New York City's population was 500,000, there were estimated to be between 10,000 to 30,000 homeless children living on the streets and in about two dozen orphanages. Something had to be done about this growing crisis. Organizations came together to birth and develop strategies and plans to deal with the enormous numbers of abandoned children.

The plan was to put these children on trains and send them across the country to families who would come to the train station in their local community to take home with them any child that was to their liking. Prior to the arrival of the train, flyers would be posted in the small towns announcing the children's arrival. Farmers would typically look for children who were healthy and able to work on the family farm. Those who looked like they came from "good stock" would be selected first. These trains came to be known as "orphan trains."

The first "orphan train" went out from The Children's Aid Society on September 20, 1854, with 46 ten-to-twelve-year-old boys and girls bound for Dowagiac, Michigan. Between 1854 and 1929, 200,000 orphaned and abandoned children traveled on orphan trains, stopping at more than 45 states across the country as well as Canada and Mexico.

This process of "distributing" these orphaned and abandoned children across the country became the predecessor to our current foster care and adoption services. Thankfully, over the last 150 years, families for the most part were able to stabilize and reduce the number of children living on the streets.

MAKING SENSE OF A LOSS OF IDENTITY AND BELONGING

But, can you imagine the thoughts and feelings that swirled in the minds and hearts of these little ones as they were loaded onto trains to be displayed across the country much like cattle going to the highest bidder? They had to feel a great sense of abandonment as well as fear of the unknown.

While not as prevalent as it was around the turn of the century, unfortunately childhood abandonment has not been totally eradicated and will never be gone completely, this side of heaven. Whenever I think of the subject of child abandonment, it grips my heart possibly more than any other issue because I have witnessed the devastating effects of these tragic occurrences.

This is what I know to be true: Abandonment appears in various forms. Realistically, any relationship can become a potential scenario for abandonment: co-workers exclude one another, parents are unwilling to provide emotional or financial support, siblings act with passive aggression, employers hire outside of the company rather than promote, spouses walk away from marriages, people choose work-career-money-success over relationships, potential retirees are pink-slipped. To add insult to injury, those who truly believed they were loved, get no support when they struggle or get the cold shoulder when they fail—no longer good enough, now alone.

Abandonment happens to all of us at some point in our lifetime.

For most of us, our first feeling of abandonment comes in early school age years when best friends choose new friends, ignore us or, even worse, pretend we never were important to them. While that abandonment scenario is hurtful when it occurs, most people adapt and move on eventually. Some children seem to simply be "thick-skinned" and it does not seem to bother them at all. Others wear their feelings on their sleeve, and it becomes very obvious their hearts are broken.

The extent of the pain from abandonment is in direct proportion to the strength of the connection in the relationship. It stands to reason that a person involved in a very close relationship will feel more pain if they are abandoned than a person would who is involved in a very superficial relationship when the abandonment takes place.

The most devastating form of abandonment I have seen over the course of my lifetime is when children are disconnected from an adult who plays a significant role in their life. The disconnect may be geographical, but emotional disconnect is enough. You know there are times when you can be there physically and be somewhere else emotionally. Both children and adults are sensitive enough to feel alone in the presence of others.

As I think about instances I have observed where children have been abandoned by the essential adults of their lives, it causes me to be consumed with feelings of sorrow and even despair on their behalf. This is just not right—it is not how our children should have to live their young lives. The unaddressed residual remains into adulthood. This happens daily in our culture as if it is normal.

Any sense of order or normalcy can turn into chaos. Our humanity says: Normalcy must be restored. Yet, the truth is "in some way, manner, or fashion" we have all experienced the loss of identity when we feel the chill that we do not belong anymore or perhaps never have—it is like the feeling we have about an inside joke we do not get once again or perhaps never have gotten. We are outside and alone.

Everyone wants to feel the security, peace, and joy of *belonging*.

BEYOND DEFENSE MECHANISMS

Defense mechanisms begin to form earlier in our lives than we realize. They appear in acting out to take control, acting out to get attention, acting out to disrupt an internal sense of helplessness, or by withdrawing to self-protect. Unaware generation after generation, we were raised by parents who use them, and we use them ourselves.

Each defense mechanism is the person's way to say, "Something is wrong here, something hurts, something must stop, someone must care enough to intervene, someone must set things right, someone beside me must be willing to agree that *enough is enough!"*

While defense mechanisms have a very significant impact on a young child's mind, emotions, and life, it is often very difficult for him to convey his feelings about what he does not comprehend. Lasting wounds to her ability to express her feelings causes her to weep over her lifetime into adulthood. That is...until someone notices and is willing to respond with intentional care.

Some children have lost a parent by death because of illness or possibly a tragic accident. Others have had a parent simply walk away from them for reasons they did not understand at the time, such as in divorce. What happens in the mind of a child in the loss of that relationship? How do children process an emotionally agonizing event of that nature?

Beginning at approximately six months old, every child experiences separation anxiety. They cry about what they cannot explain but feel instinctively. It *feels* like *abandonment* whether a parent disappears permanently or intermittently. Whenever parents personally purposefully relieve themselves of parental responsibilities, their *intentional choices* cause *the predictable effect* of abandonment in their children. Whenever parents' *personally crash* and cannot perform their parental responsibilities, their *unintentional choices* produce *the unwanted effect* of abandonment in their children.

RELEASE IS A PERSONAL DECISION

Yes, I am a woman, a wife, a mother, an aunt, and a grandmother who has been a girl, a daughter, and a sister. There is no question that I am a person who has been shaped by my perspective and the roles I have experienced. My lifetime of observations has contributed to the fact that I strongly believe that a mother is *most often* the most trusted person in a person's life, but I would be remiss if I did not say that this *should be equally true* of fathers.

Biblically speaking, the role and relationship with each parent was designed by God to have an intentional result. Both parents are *needed* to be *most trusted, most loving ones.* We were meant to gain at least healthy *development, character, and support* from our mothers and gain at least healthy *security, motivation, and confidence* from our fathers, each one contributing to the effectiveness of the other. You might notice that many people are desperately lacking these developmental benefits all over the world. The absence of either parent plays a major role in the potential stunting of our becoming the people who God created us to be.

In my wildest imagination, I cannot even fathom ever abandoning my children, grandchildren, niece, or nephews. Yet, again, in our culture, mothers do abandon those they have literally birthed. There may be a plethora of *personal* reasons a person may give for abandoning their children *geographically* or *emotionally.* However, in my mind, it is unconscionable.

I do understand there may be instances (i.e. teenage pregnancies) when a child may be better off to be adopted by a family that can love and care for them. I do not consider this abandonment. I consider a choice like this to be loving action for the long-term benefit and welfare of a child. The birth mother in these circumstances is making *a heroic decision for the good of the child*—the goal is to provide a loving home with parents who will willingly take on the full responsibilities of parenthood and have the wherewithal to create a fulfilling life for the child. It is one *very early* personal decision to *release.*

In some of the discussions I have had with my grandchildren and my niece, I have asked them, "What things would you *not* want to have happen to you?" Interestingly, one response was *abandonment.* I then asked, "What does this word mean to you and how does it make you feel?" All of them responded individually with a single word: *loneliness.* Loneliness is something no one likes to experience.

We have been created for relationship with others and we all have a need to feel loved, accepted, and valued. The *belonging* environment of Family Life is the place carefully designed by God so that each person might have the opportunity to experience this. What we know is meant to be true must be responsibly restored by each of us. "What we missed by dysfunction" *CAN BE HEALED* by *Fighting FOR Our FAMILY Together! Feel the HOPE! With God, it's not too late!*

LOVED, ACCEPTED, AND VALUED

Even if a child infrequently sees a parent who has abandoned them, the absence of real love, compassion, and acceptance expressed by the parent only reinforces this sense of loneliness. A parent can say things to their child to address the *disconnection* between them—for example, "I love you" and "I want to come back" and "I want to be with you." Yet, a child may not *feel loved, accepted, or valued.*

Your child, at any age (from 1 to 101), will find it impossible to *believe the words* that are being spoken because they always feel like something is wrong, feel like they have done something wrong, feel like they will never be forgiven, feel like they are invisible, or feel like no matter what they do it is never enough. Words can be empty and hollow while a person's actions will actually tell the real story. To quote an old adage, "Your actions speak louder than your words."

Even though loving family members may step in to try to take the place of absentee parents, there is still a void. While the other parent, grandparents, sisters, brothers, aunts, uncles, or cousins try to fill the emptiness left by the abandoning parent, they are never able to truly replace *the love a child needs to feel from both mother and father.* Sadly, many children do not experience *the blessing of a caring extended family* fighting *FOR* them!

Whole books are written about the deep effects healthy or unhealthy parenting has on every other relationship we experience, *especially* marriage. A dysfunctional unhealthy lack of *development, character, support, security, motivation, and confidence* takes its toll on everyone. But *we can choose to disbelieve lies* that claim we cannot *change,* cannot *make a difference,* and cannot *have the life* we were created by God to LIVE!

OWNING THE REALITY

When children go to school and tell their friends they live with one parent or their grandparents, or they live in a foster home, *their friends often understand only because broken families have become commonplace in our society.* It is *not unusual* to hear these stories.

Children usually *do not have to explain*, "Well, my mom abandoned us when we were very young and it is not that we do not see her, but we do not see her very often. We live with my Dad and my grandparents. They take care of us during the daytime. We see Dad every day when he comes home from work and are with him on weekends."

This fractured-home scenario continues to exist because parents still do not want to, do not know how to, or do not have the tools or role modeling to take responsibility for their own children. There is an empty space inside them that has never been filled or a tool never handed on to them.

Children who experience the abandonment of a parent will undoubtedly be affected in their adult life. What will happen to these children when they become young adults? How will they make decisions regarding marriage? How will they treat their spouse? How will they respond to the responsibilities of parenthood when they begin to have children of their own? How will they treat their children? How will they respond to their children?

Will this abandonment issue be perpetuated into the next generation? Realistically, only time will tell. But WE CAN say no, mean no, be unwilling to accept the effects of abandonment by making new healthy choices that replace the choices of our past! This is The FIGHT FOR FAMILY WE were meant to CHOOSE AND WIN!

The teens I talked to who *were not abandoned by a parent* could not even fathom how a parent could leave their children. For them, it was not even an issue. But the teens who *were abandoned by a parent* understood they would have parental responsibilities they must handle if they were ever to become a parent. For them, it was a real issue and one to which they had already given thought. One even indicated that *not having children* was a potential choice, thereby avoiding the parental responsibility altogether. I responded, "That would be a great loss for you. You are such a loving, caring, precious spirit that you would be an amazing parent."

REGAINING POWER BEGINS AND GROWS

One of my granddaughters explained her experience saying: "It has been seventeen years and yet it still feels temporary. When I was three, my brother, sister, and I were taken away from our parents, and our grandmother took over the job of caring for us. It was supposed to be for a couple of weeks to allow my parents to get back on their feet but, as the days, weeks, and years went by, it became more and more permanent.

As a three-year-old, there was a lot of confusion, although *today* I remember the details *vividly*. At times I loved to just go back and remember the 'good old days', the days of being 'normal' in a 'normal family'. At other times, I hated to remember. I wanted to forget what had happened because this was my family now—me, my sister, my brother, and my strong grandmother.

All that mattered was that we had each other; we were not *alone.* We had to figure it out and get used to having our parents *in and out* of our lives. They were never *ready* to settle down and take care of a child—let alone triplets. The change at such a young age was hard but settling down was not going to be easy; it all happened so fast. My grandmother had chosen to move back to Texas to take care of us. That meant she was not just a grandmother on her own, but a single mother as well.

Growing up, I had a hard time dealing with the fact that my parents were not *around*—we all did. I remember my sister crying to a song we used to listen to with Mom before bed every night. That was when I knew I needed to *step up* for them and I became very mature and responsible at a young age. I tried to help my brother and my sister cope with their pain *the only way I knew how*—by shutting out everything around me that I loved. At least, I tried to convince myself that I could. But they were hurting, and so was I. *I was scared to love* something when it was at risk of being *temporary.*"

BY RELEASING CONTROL

"I felt that I needed to *stay strong* for them and for my grandmother who had given up so much for us. I felt the burden on my shoulders, and I think they did too. She tried so hard. None of us wanted to make her *feel like* she was not good enough or appreciated, because she was. She tried her best to get us as involved as possible, from signing us up for every activity they offered at the YMCA to supporting our school activities. She tried her best to steer our focus onto other things to help us discover our interests and passions. She also wanted us to realize the opportunities we had— that we could *make something* of ourselves and *take charge* of our lives.

Although I did not feel *that* way, *I sensed a loss of control* in my life; I was *lost. I aimed to control everything around me,* and I surrendered all my focus to the idea that we were different. I wanted so badly to *be like* other families where words like "Mom" and "Dad" did not sound foreign to my ears. Despite this, I knew no matter how hard I tried to *control* it, I could not *change* the fact that we were not. From there, since I could not *control* my home life, I figured I would *focus all my attention* on my interests, passions, academics, and cheering, which grew to become *the center of my future.* I began to develop *anxiety* which began to take over my life. I was *scared* to do *one* thing wrong. I made sure to double check everything that I did because I felt my *future* was in jeopardy if I did not.

Throughout the years, I have grown to realize that *I was wrong.* I have learned that *no one's perfect, no one's family* is perfect, and *no one's LIFE* is perfect. No matter how much you try to *control* it, that is where the *normal* is. Everything happens for a reason and going through all this has left me stronger and more determined to make something of myself. That is what keeps me going!"

UNLEARNING THE GRIP OF CONTROL

Sometimes children learn *what not to do* from their parents. I am convinced this is one of those times. While no one knows the future, I have a high degree of confidence that these children will learn not to make the choices that created their parents' circumstances. *Our children should learn from our mistakes.* We should admit them, apologize for them, and learn from them. *We should also learn from our children.* We should unlearn the grip of control and release control TOGETHER! We should REGAIN POWER as a FAMILY to live the lives we were created to live TOGETHER!

What about your children? Is there any form of abandonment you have displayed toward them? Are you showing up (present and accounted for)? Are you there when they need you? Do you take time to hug them? Do play catch with them in the backyard? Do you have "pretend tea parties" with them? Do you *talk with them*, not just chit-chat or ask for information? Do you ask them, "Am I giving you everything you need? Do you need more from me?"

In turn, do you ask young adults for what you need as a parent or guardian? Do you show them you love them in the ways *they need and want to be loved?* Do they *believe* you when you *tell* them you love them *because your actions match your words?*

How do we break the potential cycle of abandonment?

WE show up!

We become godly examples to our children.

Your children are the most important gift God has entrusted to you in this life.

Do not abandon them to any degree in any way.

Show them how important they are by being there for them—

by doing what is right to make the difference you alone can make.

Show up at every passage and every turn of their life!

Show them how to be a good parent so they will be able to do the same.

I am convinced that godly counsel is the key to successful families. We find it in *the changeless Truth taught in God's Word (The Bible).* From it, we will learn how to trust His Presence and Power within us to produce and display the kind of loving, caring, compassionate example God intends for us to be for our children and the generations to come! We will learn how to *release control to God and gain His power to win The Fight FOR FAMILY!*

You can be the father your children respect or the mother they adore.

I pray that your children will rise up and call you blessed!

WE CAN leave a legacy of abundance and freedom to our descendants and to the world!

Defeating Generational Dysfunction, Finding Generational Freedom

Three Empowering Principles with Three Equipping Questions to Fight FOR YOUR FAMILY

CHAPTER EIGHT

Principle One. We step out of control when we trust God to be God.

Scripture: Proverbs 3:5-6 (NIV) "Trust in the Lord with all your heart and lean not on your own understanding; in all your ways acknowledge Him, and He will make your paths straight."

Explanation: People have been tempted by the enemy for centuries to distrust God. To trust God means that we believe Him. To trust God means that we know He knows. To trust God means that we acknowledge His presence, protection, and provision. To trust God means that He will direct us and straighten out crooked paths. To trust God means that we do not have to be in control because we know that He is in control and taking care of us.

Question 1.
Which parts of trusting God do you struggle with most?

Question 2.
Because God is present everywhere, what places in your life do you tend not to see Him? What places do you find yourself trying to get and keep control because you believe you must?

Question 3.
Where will you begin to release to Him the control that truly has always been His?

Principle Two. We step into reality when we believe He is always working.

Scripture: Romans 8:28 (NLT) "...we know that God causes everything to work together for the good of those who love God and are called according to His purpose for them."

Explanation: People tend to want to get all their ducks in a row. We tend to want to coordinate everything so that everything works out perfectly. There comes a time when we admit that we cannot maintain order for the world. We begin to see that God is God without our help, yet He chooses to work with us, through us, and for us. He is Sovereignly at work on our behalf, yet He chooses to do through us as His partners what we alone were created to do which is "our part".

Question 1.

Releasing control is surrender, not asking for assistance. What control do you struggle to release? Why?

Question 2.

The world says, "If it's to be, it's up to me". What would make you want to reply, "If it is to be, it is up to God Who also works through me"?

Question 3.

Where must you begin to choose to believe He is working so that He can show you that He is?

Principle Three. We step into power when we recognize His presence within.

Scripture: Galatians 2:20-21 (NLT)

"My old self has been crucified with Christ. It is no longer I who live, but Christ lives in me. So, I live in this earthly body by trusting in the Son of God, who loved me and gave Himself for me."

Explanation: People want to ask God to help "them do it". God wants us to let "Him do it" through us. The Holy Spirit of Christ present within us is our life and is our power to live life. Because we cannot see inside ourselves, our biggest task is to remember to recognize His presence. This is not easy, but it is the secret to regaining power we think we have lost. When we recognize His presence, we gain access to His power to live and to do the part that is ours to do. The rest is His.

Question 1.

Why would you wrongly believe that you must do what only God can do and why would you try?

Question 2.

What will begin to change when you begin to ask God to show you your part and let Him do it through you?

Question 3.

How do you think things will be different when you acknowledge His presence inside you? What new choices will you be making since you are not abandoned?

Chapter Nine
TRUST YOUR CREATOR'S OPINION

You can get to *the Heart of everything in creation* when you know what is in *your Creator's Heart.* There is not one thing in all of creation that is missing the signature fingerprint of God. *His finest work is in the intricate details* of what He has created and who He has created. It is in those details that *He reveals His heart* for this beautiful broken world.

The very One Who creates by His words calls what He desires into being. That is how the Biblical historian describes creation's manifestation out of nothing. In each of the first five days of creation, each thing that was created was created in *correlation* with another creation to sustain it and support it. But on the sixth day, He created *people*—He *designed* us to be in *relationship with Him* as our lifelong Companion and Perfecter.

In Psalm 139:13-18[22], the Creator's Heart is expressed through the Psalmist when he writes:

For You fashioned my inmost being, you knit me together in my
mother's womb.
I thank You because I am awesomely made, wonderfully;
Your works are wonders — I know this very well.
My bones were not hidden from You when I was being made in
secret,
intricately woven in the depths of the earth.

Your eyes could see me as an embryo, but in Your book all my
days were already written;
my days had been shaped before any of them existed.
God, how I prize Your thoughts! How many of them there are!
If I count them, there are more than grains of sand; if I finish the
count, I am still with You.

THE ONE WHO KNOWS YOU BEST

Our Creator knows us BEST. God knows what we need. He knows
we need *to know and feel... that we are loved, understood, and valued
for even the smallest of our unique details.* Equally amazing to me is
that God is willing and able to use all His creation to reveal the full
measure of His love for every human being. That is the kind of God
that we can know and serve!

As for His creation, I am especially fond of four-legged animals.
I am convinced that when a soul has been deeply wounded there's
nothing quite as healing as the unconditional love of a dog or a cat
or a pig or a horse. I have loved and learned from all God's creatures.

BRITTANY

I have this picture of my granddaughter Brittany when she was
a young girl that would just take your breath away if you could see
it. It is one of my all-time favorite photos of that sweet girl. For as
long as I can remember, Brittany has loved horses like few people
on this earth. The photo shows her with her gorgeous quarter-horse

Nikko whose leg is wrapped completely around her as though he is pulling her into his embrace. Brittany's whole young body is nestled in as close as he can possibly bring her. I have never seen such a tender display of compassion from such a sizable horse to a young girl who desperately needed a few extra ounces of love. *Only God knew she would find such joy and fulfillment connecting with horses—* not only in the riding, but in the loving and caring for them and for all those who were created to have horses in their lives. *He knows us all so well.*

Each time I see that photo I think to myself, "If God came to earth as a horse, this is what His love for Brittany would look like." I think, because she loves horses so much and being around them makes her feel *safe*, God gave her this photographed moment as if to say, "Brittany, never forget *how much I love you.* I know what makes you tick because I created you, My child. You are remarkably *unique.* If you ever forget how much I really love you, pull out this photo—you are loved *just the way you are!*"

NO ONE KNOWS ME BETTER

As for me, I must admit it seems like I have been a dog lover all my life—since the very day I left my mother's womb. Like children, I can name them all: Buddy Bear, Boo, Kirby, Katie Sugarbaker, John Norman Howard, Buffy, Papa, Sofie Tucker, Desi, one adorable blue-eyed cat named Kitty Frankie, and a pot-bellied pig named Bonna. When people have gone from me, failed me, or left me alone, *God designed each one of these adorable creatures just for me*!

Those dogs, that one cat, and the pot-bellied pig have *always* arrived just on time in the very season of my life when I needed them most. Whether I am happy or sad or anything in between, without wavering those animals have been able to discern whatever is going on inside me in an uncanny way. They seem to know my every high and every low and respond appropriately in every situation.

Honestly, *I have never been without God.* Yet, He has provided companionship through those precious four-legged creatures to *let me know* just how loved I am. Truly, God's opinion of me has been shown to me, time and time again, through the expressions of their unconditional love. Through them, I sense that *I am His cherished daughter.* Sometimes, one look of adoration will be all I need. At other times, it is a quiet whimper that communicates that, whether I am at my worst or doing my "daily darndest" to give my best, God loves me *unreservedly.*

What I am really trying to drive home is that *every one of us* is a unique creation of God. By His design, each one of us has different needs and different gifts—*no one knows us better than our Maker.* Just saying—when we get this down deep in our bones, the opinions of others about our lives and how we measure up will never hold us down or hold us back. When we really get this, we will begin to recognize *how He works in our lives through all the things* that *make us uniquely us.*

In and through Brittany, God uses horses to reveal His love and to bring out her very best. When she is working with a horse, there is no denying the giftings and abilities He has placed in her—she lights up like a harvest moon!

CUSTOM MADE FAMILY

Here is what I see when I observe my family: Though we come from the same family, each of us is so different. *We are all custom made*—not one of us is alike. We are more than different. We are unique. I love the way that 1st Corinthians 12:4-6,11[23] explains our uniqueness:

> [4]There are different kinds of spiritual gifts, but the same Spirit is the source of them all.
> [5]There are different kinds of service, but we serve the same Lord.
> [6]God works in different ways, but it is the same God who does the work in all of us.
> [11] It is the one and only Spirit who distributes all these gifts. He alone decides which gift each person should have.

And, why is all this upfront just-for-you in this chapter? Because you already know that the opinions of people shape our perception of ourselves and dictate our own internal-endless-loop of self-criticism and doubt. All the *"could haves, should haves,* and *would haves"* of other people and their opinions damage our daily progress, dampen our daily hope, dilute our daily joy, and do have the potential to undermine our future legacy.

But, my gosh, if we truly understood that no one (including ourselves) knows us better than our Maker, then we would realize that *the only opinion that really matters* is *the opinion of The One Who made us!* He has not only created each of us unique, but *for a one-of-a-kind Divinely designed purpose!*

THE COMPARISON GAME

Most of the time, we are just too busy *comparing ourselves* to discover who we uniquely are or Whose we are—we *belong to Him*. So, we just end up listening to the opinions of others who only know about us what we show them. The world is so quick to whisper in our ears: "you should have done this, you ought to do that, you could have done it better, if only you would have done it that way." Truly, it is awfully painful and deeply sad that, if we listen long enough, in a short time we lose sight of the opinion of The One Who loves us most.

O my friends, *comparison* is a dangerous game. The Scripture warns us not to compare our lives to anyone else. Galatians 6:4 says, "Let each person *examine* his own work, and then he can take pride in himself *alone*, and *not compare himself with someone else*"[24] . To compare our story to another's story is to deny the unique story that God has written for each of our lives.

Nevertheless, in today's social-media-driven world, to lose sight of The One Whose opinion matters most is an easier thing to lose than ever before. If you spend any amount of time scrolling through Facebook, Instagram, Snapchat or Pinterest, there is a good chance that it will not be long before you too will be measuring yourself against every half-told story or air-brushed picture-perfect moment that may not even be the truth.

Now, I am betting you understand the seriousness of this matter and that perhaps you have already seen this playout in hurtful or destructive ways, just as I have. Maybe someone you love has experienced a snub, a rejection, or a put down which has hurt your heart—especially if it is your child or a child you know. You see that look in their eyes, that flicker of pain, and lately see how they hesitate to chime in or share their opinions, hopes, or dreams. Slighted one too many times, they withdraw internally because it is too risky to reveal their true soul to other human beings.

Indeed, they may show up for group functions, because it is the polite and expected thing to do to be present at a family gathering or workplace event. But inside, they are hurting before they arrive and unsure of their true worth and value because somewhere along the way the opinions of others began to overshadow the opinion of The One Who knows them best.

THE RIGHT QUESTION, THE RIGHT ANSWER

The War we are fighting began in the Garden when our Enemy first asked the question: "Did God really say ..."[25] The answer is YES, He did! When we know the right question, the right answer is ours! God created you to BE someone with a unique purpose and mission!

As parents and grandparents, it is more critical than ever that *we close the opinion gap* and zero in with the children and our grandchildren on the question: *"WHO did God create you to BE?"*

From the time when we are small children, all of us at one time are another have been asked: "WHAT do you want to be when you grow up?" And then, to complicate matters even more, people who *really don't know us* project their opinions onto us too, saying "you should *be* this or you should *do* that." The truth of the matter is that, somewhere along the way, we started asking the wrong question because we were never taught to ask *"God, who did You create me to be?"*

When we ask the wrong question, we get the wrong answer— every time. We need to have healthy discussions with children and grandchildren—talking together openly and honestly about the way

God created us to be, telling them how we sometimes waste valuable years and opportunities when we compare ourselves to others, when we fail to realize who we were created to be, when we let the opinions of others overshadow the opinion of The One Who knows us best.

Because, this is Reality—The Father, the Maker of us all, has the answer we need. He knows exactly who and what He created us to be. And He loves us so much that, even when we make a mess of our years and opportunities, He will restore our lives—if *we* just *ASK Him!*

Take Abraham for example. It appeared to him that he had made a total mess of everything, even after being promised that he and his wife Sarah would have a child. Yes, they took matters into their own hands and made an historical mess. But God! God took Abraham out under the stars and basically said to him, "'Take a look at all the stars! I know you think you have ruined everything, but I promise you this—your children will number more than all the stars in the sky'[26]. I know you are sorry, and I have all of this ... because now I have all of you! I have a plan for your life, and I will bring to fruition everything I have created you to be."

There is just something about *the father-child relationship!* I love being a mom, aunt, and grandmother; would not want it any other way. But I also love watching the interaction between fathers and their children—especially when a father lends his own strength to a child that is struggling. It is *a thing of great beauty!*

BROOKE

My oldest grandchild Brooke was recently asked, "Who is the person that has most helped you in your life?"

Without skipping a beat, Brooke said, "My Dad. He has always looked for the good in me. He has always been there for me. Like back when I was so unhappy in school, sometimes even skipping school, when most parents would have freaked out and grounded their kids, my dad took what I had to say seriously.

He listened to my sadness and heard me when I said I was not comfortable at my current school. He invested in me and paid for me to go to another school that I really wanted to attend. My Dad respected me and treated me like an adult. And yes, I know there were times that I needed to be disciplined, but he always disciplined in a way that never made me feel like I wanted to push him away. He was patient with me in a difficult season. Somehow God knew I needed a dad like him! None of us are perfect, but we all need someone to believe in us."

Living in a fallen imperfect world, I love Brooke's response—gratefulness—for an imperfect dad who loved her despite her imperfections. It doesn't get much better than that this side of heaven because this is what I know to be true—there is not a parent anywhere who does not have regrets. I marvel that God can use us, imperfections and all, to love our children. Even when we are far from perfect, He redeems our mishandlings just like He did for Abraham.

Lately my prayer has been:

"Cover all the times that we have mishandled Your blessings and grant us grace to love one other through the difficult places.
And, may my children and grandchildren
seek only the opinion of The One Who loves them most.
Set them free from the grip of the opinions of others

that would keep them from flourishing in all that You have created them to be."

ENOUGH IS ENOUGH

Yes, for me—*Enough is enough!* I am throwing down the gauntlet. I want an "AFTER" picture that replaces *our* "BEFORE" picture. I want a better after picture for *myself,* for *all those I love,* and for *all those my life influences, including a better after picture for* YOU. That better after picture comes from *learning to trust the opinion of The One Who knows us best, The One Who created each of us!*

Whose opinion we trust begins to be shaped not long after we leave the womb. Early words *spoken* and intentional attention *shown* as a child develops ... establishes their character, shapes their personality, and sets coordinates for their journey through life.

People who only see the glass half empty tend to raise children to see the glass half empty. This is about those frequent *"coulda, shoulda, wouldas"* which our culture has made famously commonplace. When my report is: "I have all As and one B". Your reaction is: "You could have, you should have, you would have done better, if...!" Perfection, even though it is a moving target, is typically rewarded. It is as if progress is essentially immaterially nothing.

THE FATHER GOD CONNECTION

The results of years of an increasing absence of fathers in the lives of their children has proven that what fathers say *with words and deeds* is so very important to each child. If a father's character, encouragement, support, demonstration, and approval are missing, a child's healthy growth is damaged.

But that child's healthy growth is not beyond repair when the child comes to know The Father Who creates each child, provides for each child, and has planned a great future for each child.

Fathers who treat their children as God treats us can be part of that accelerated effective healing process by speaking and acting the way God does—treating each child as a Masterpiece.

We are *AT WAR*. We always have been, even when *UNAWARE* was our normal. If we are wise, if we are strong, if we are right, we are FIGHTING *FOR* FAMILY. Now, we are wiser, stronger, and *"righter"* than ever before. And yet, *our family's best is yet to be!*

The stakes are raised as each of us get older. Time becomes more and more valuable as it passes. The stakes are raised as we get healthier. We are opposed by the jealous when we make progress.

As parents and children, brothers and sisters, and true friends, we can reflect the heart of our Creator. His words and actions can become *ours*. *Our* words and actions can encourage *us* to trust His opinion and design. *Our* words and actions can do the *same* for others.

This is not a *TELL-ALL* book! ...it is a *HEAL-ALL* book!

This book is about the fact that all of us have had *an undesirable before picture* and all of us can have the opportunity to have *an ever improving after picture!*

We want your children and grandchildren to know that *God is in the details* and He cares about their hearts. His opinion is He created His children to heal and WIN!

Brittany Willis

Defeating Generational Dysfunction, Finding Generational Freedom

Three Empowering Principles with Three Equipping Questions to Fight FOR YOUR FAMILY

CHAPTER NINE

Principle One. We choose our best life when we honor our Creator.

Scripture: Psalm 139:13-14 (NLT) "For You created my inmost being; You knit me together in my mother's womb. I praise You because I am fearfully and wonderfully made; Your works are wonderful; I know that full well."

Explanation: The very best way to make the most of life is to be authentically who we were created to be, nothing more, nothing less. It is the highest form of honor when we say to God "Your plan for me and opinion of me matters most to me. My opinion of You changes everything." The war waged against this (through the opinion of others) begins early in life. So, it is a war that must be learned, if it is to be personally won. But you can win the war by choosing to honor Him.

Question 1.

No matter what has happened so far, it is not too late to make God's opinion your opinion. What opinions will you have to begin to tackle first to get started?

Question 2.

Where will you have to look to hear and know God's opinion? Who can help you zero in on it?

Question 3.

To value the unique way you were made, you will have to begin to believe God makes no mistakes. How will you now need to see your past and who you have been so far...to be able to succeed?

Principle Two. We are created to contribute. Life is not all about us.

Scripture: 1 Corinthians 12:4, 11 (NLT) "There are different kinds of spiritual gifts, but the same Spirit is the source of them all. ... 11 It is the one and only Spirit who distributes all these gifts. He alone decides which gift each person should have."

Explanation: Like a body part uniquely performs its role, each of us have been Creator designed to be Holy Spirit empowered in a way that no one else can be. Our configuration of gifts, passion, abilities, personality, and experiences make our contribution priceless. No one can take that reality away from you. But the opinions of others can diminish your belief and function when you try to be someone you are not. Only you can be you and their lives are not ultimately dependent on us.

Question 1.

What have you been tempted to try to be that you know you are not?

Question 2.

How much effort have you made to get a clear picture from God on why He created you?

Question 3.

What will it take to become the best version of you that you can be? How will God's opinion reshape and teach you?

Principle Three. We must become God pleasers to be our best.

Scripture: Galatians 1:10 (NLT) "Obviously, I'm not trying to win the approval of people, but of God. If pleasing people were my goal, I would not be Christ's servant.

Explanation: The ongoing cultural temptation is to blend into the current norm. It is disillusioning because what is current is always changing. You were meant to grow, not morph. God wants you to be secure in knowing who He has created you to be. He does not change His expectations based on situations like people do. He empowers you to be that unique creation who enters the world to transform it into all it can be! When God is pleased, you will be too!

Question 1.

Whose opinions create imbalance in your life. How can your unique genuine contribution make things better for them because you have something great to offer?

Question 2.

How will being secure that you are pleasing God affect you, when people who are focused on themselves come and go?

Question 3.

How will the appreciation, confidence, support, and belief in you which comes from your Creator Who is your eternal Father affect your opinion of yourself and drive you forward?

Chapter Ten
VALUE YOUR UNIQUENESS, APPRECIATE YOUR DIFFERENCES

There is a war going on out there made up of *enemy thieves who want to steal our identities. Their strategy is to make us believe* we cannot be *authentic*, we must blend in by *compromise*, and we are alive to make others happy by *fulfilling their wishes and needs*. So, it should not surprise me that …

The journey of writing this book has taken much longer than I ever imagined.

But in this God-ordained holy pause, this divine delay, I have been given a most wonderful gift—a front row seat to the unfolding *differences* of each grandchild—who surely have their different personalities, interests, abilities, strengths and issues. They are all becoming *successful* at being themselves and in their relationships.

So why is this such a big deal? Because, as my friend Mark Williams teaches, until you value your uniqueness and the uniqueness of others, you cannot fully appreciate the differences of one another. Without valuing our *"uniqueness's"*, we will never experience the joy of being fully alive with one another. *To be fully alive* only occurs when we come together as a whole family, a whole church, a whole community, a whole organization and allow our differences to make us complete. Without those differences, we are somehow *less* than whole.

VARIETY IS THE SPICE OF LIFE

I have been giving this a great deal of thought. So, I will use an illustration to make this more relevant, because I do not want you to miss the vital truth of *appreciating our differences.*

If I were to invite you to share my favorite meal, Thanksgiving dinner, which is my all-time favorite holiday and I said, "Please come be our guest and share our dinner—we are having buttered carrots!" And then I left it at that—offering no further information than that we are having carrots, how excited would you be? You probably would be less than thrilled. You might even think to yourself, "Carrots? Buttered Carrots? Is that the meal? Just carrots?"

But what if I were to say, "We are going to have buttered carrots, but not just buttered, they will be sprinkled with a little bit of brown sugar and other savory flavors. The turkey will be brined and cooked on an open pit. We will have homemade yeast rolls, fresh baked. When you walk through our front door, the smell of those rolls will make your mouth water right then and there. The coffee will be freshly ground. The garden-fresh corn, sliced right off the cobb, will be placed in a beautiful serving bowl where you can take as many spoonful's as your heart desires. Please fill your plate to the brim. And there is more...we are going to have mashed potatoes. But not just any mashed potatoes. We are going to have red-skinned smashed potatoes with pressed garlic, grass-fed butter and sour cream. Those potatoes will melt in your mouth and you will wish that you were not swallowing so fast *because* you will want to *savor* every bite.

Or, we *could* just have those carrots. We will bring some in from California, some in from New Jersey, some in from Florida and we will bring some in from Louisiana. But essentially, we are having carrots. And they are going to be *buttered*. That is the *whole* meal, but they will be great carrots!!!!" Now, how ridiculous would that be?

OUR DIFFERENCES COMPLETE US

To say "we want carrots only" is like saying *everybody must be* a carrot. And if we are all carrots, then everybody just must be slender with a little green tuft on top. We will not have to worry about a tan because we will all turn orange. And yes, we will have the same specific vitamins and minerals, but we will also be seriously deficient in everything else. But my gosh, we will be *good* carrots!

Oh, and did I forget to mention that at the *whole* meal, the *real* meal, there also will be pie—with a pecan cookie crust served warm with a scoop of vanilla ice cream? And, I think by now you are getting the picture...

Real joy and complete wholeness come not just in the discovery of our own uniqueness and/or sameness, but in the appreciation of our differences too. When we *welcome* our differences to the table, *we become* "like the best thanksgiving meal ever"—a meal abundant in a variety of flavors, colors and scrumptiousness—lacking nothing because everything that is needed to bring out the best in all of us is gathered around the table. It is only when we acknowledge and welcome our differences that we flourish as a family, as a church, as an organization. *Our differences are what make us whole.*

Can you imagine if you were scheduled to attend a conference and you were so excited to participate because of all the people that you were going to meet whose gifts and talents could change your world, improve your relationships and better your business? 4,000 people are scheduled to attend. As you make your way into the convention hall, you are so excited. But, then to your disappointment you discover that there are 3,999 people exactly like you. How helpful would that be? It would not be helpful at all! Nor would it be fun, energizing, or *desirably* memorable. We must embrace and cherish the differences in order to know completeness.

In 1st Corinthians 12:17[27] the Apostle Paul summarizes everything I have been saying in one verse:

"If the whole body were an eye, how could it hear; if we were all hearing, how could we smell?"

WORTH THE EFFORT

As a grandmother, aunt, and woman who is now feeling the seasons, it has been my greatest joy to observe the unfolding of our differences because, at this point, it is no longer about how we bring our uniqueness to the table—it is also about how we are learning to contribute to each other through our differences, not only to help one another, but to take joy in one another!

For twenty-five years, I have cherished every Thanksgiving as the family has gathered around our table. But this Thanksgiving, with the writing of this book, I am keenly aware that our differences are what make our family precious and whole. It does not mean that these differences come without challenges but this I can most certainly say:

As I picture the faces of my family, my husband, our children, niece, nephews, and grandchildren—I *see* what they bring to the table and *want* to acknowledge that our family would be incomplete without *all* our beautiful differences. We *make* each other better.

My husband Mike Willis, Sr. has a faith and vision that surpasses anything I have ever known. I am overwhelmed by his love for the Lord, his family, and his life's work. Honestly, I cannot hear the words of *"The Battle Hymn of The Republic"*[28] without thinking of my husband: "He has sounded forth the trumpet that shall never call retreat, He is sifting out the hearts of men before His judgment seat; O, be swift, my soul, to answer Him, be jubilant, my feet! Our God is marching on."

That is the way Mike Willis wants to and has sought to lead our family—with the hand of God upon him. I am forever grateful for his strong leadership. *It goes without saying, both Mike and I made mistakes and have regrets. It is my prayer* that both Mike and I be found faithful in the challenges that arise everyday as husband and wife, father and mother, uncle and aunt, grandfather and grandmother. Our deepest desire is that *the best of both of us* will influence generations of our family for years to come.

Our grown children also bring their incredible differences to our table. How incomplete our family would be without our differences. We would not be whole; we would not be complete. We are a *blended family.*

When Mike and I married in 1977, I had one daughter, and he had two sons from his first marriage and one daughter from his second marriage. Within two weeks of Mike and I being married, his first wife began to travel. Mike Jr. moved in with us when he was eight years old. Mark was nine when he came a year and half later. My daughter Tammy was eight years old. The kids remained with us until they graduated college.

But here is what I want you know, *the hardest thing* about raising our kids *was remembering my past because I did not want the kids to make the same mistakes I had made.* I wanted better for them, but *I had so much to learn.* My mother once told me, "Francie, even if you fall, you can always fall forward. Deep water is where the fish really are." Yet, I hardly knew what I was doing with one child, much less with three full-time kids. After all, I was a newlywed. And it was hard taking on the new role of stepmother and the new role of wife to a man destined for fame and fortune.

OUR BEAUTIFUL DIFFERENCES 1.0

In writing this book, *I had one goal: I wanted to know and tell how a family is healed from dysfunction.* And in writing this book, I have had the privilege of recollecting past moments, days, months, and the years of these precious four children.

I see more clearly than ever that each one of them has brought beautiful memories into my life. Each one has brought something different to the table—distinctive and worthy of *appreciation.* These are their differences which I share so that you too might learn to recognized and embrace the differences around your own table of love and experience wholeness and completeness within your family.

Tammy is "*my let me do it my way—advice seldom taken kind of girl*". Her motto is "*let me learn the hard way, if I want to*". She was born on Easter morning and was the answer to my heart's deepest longing. I wanted a baby girl because, in truth, I could not imagine what I would do with a boy or how I could possibly be a good mother to boys without knowing anything about boys. So, I prayed hard for that baby girl. She was and still is adorable and precious to me from the first moment I laid eyes on her. She is the most loving and caring daughter, mother, sister, and friend anyone could have.

Mike Jr. is "*my easy breezy about life boy*". Oh, how I love that about him! Honestly, not much ever upsets Mike. He is so funny and always makes us laugh—especially me. There are so many things about him that remind me of me—it is uncanny. He talks to himself just like I have always done. I believe I laugh at *just listening to him* as much as *I laugh at all his many antics.* He would tell you that our favorite words for each other are *love* and *goofy*. Michael has had a hard life—he turned left when he should have turned right—but I am happy to say that *he is on the up and up and I am cheering wildly for him.*

Mark is "*my filibuster type of guy*". He was born to be a great politician. He loves debate and he is still someone who will debate a topic until you will likely just have to say, "I give up!" (even if you do not agree with what he has to say). God *gifted* Mark with this *talent*. I wanted Mark to go up East to a political school. However, he was always a great athlete and loved to play basketball. Therefore, *he chose* a college prep school in Arkansas that *he knew he could* help get a State Championship. And, *he did. Determination is Mark's strongest attribute* and it has taken him a long way.

These three kids living beneath our roof had to learn how to be a family. Tammy and I had been on our own for a long time. Mike Jr. and Mark had never lived with a sister. Needless to say, we were *not* exactly *the Brady Bunch*. There were tensions as they grew towards becoming a sister and brothers. But, in time, they learned to respect and appreciate each other as they matured. The sweetest thing of all is that, when they each left for college, they missed each other.

Deborah is *"my enjoy life to the fullest kind of girl"*. As Mike's youngest daughter, Deborah never lived in our home, but spent weekends, holidays, and summer vacation with us—that is *where most* of my memories of her were made! She has always been *so bright* and *just fun* to be around. She receives joy out of everything. Her laughter is real and infectious.

My heart is full when I think about how much more God has planned for our children in years to come, and how much farther *we can choose to go together* ...

WHEN DIFFERENCES DIVIDE, PRAY

Do you remember how I said, "the hardest thing of all about raising our kids was remembering my past and that I did not want them to make the same mistakes"?

Well, here is the reason: for generations, *our family has been riddled with various forms of dysfunction* that have come from excessive drinking and other forms of addiction. *I did not want my children to struggle with any of those things.* No parent ever does. Yet, we live in this very fallen world and, in almost every family I know, dysfunction has impacted most of us.

Our children have had to *battle their own* forms of dysfunction and addiction. It has been *agonizing* to watch them struggle at times. But I am thankful that, for the most part, we have been able to come alongside of them out of our deep desire to provide the tools and support we *all* need to become *victorious* in our life choices. If we were successful at anything, we encouraged them to build strong families which I believe has helped them reclaim their stability.

As I take a step back and look at the landscape of our differences, I see each person love and defend their families ferociously. However, they have had disagreements and family issues with each other from time to time. Who has not? Yes, it is disappointing when we mistreat each other, feelings are hurt, grudges are held, and apologies are not given.

In those moments, I hit my knees and ask God for a *fresh outpouring* of compassion and forgiveness to fall like gentle rain upon our family, because families should lift up and not let down. Families should value the unique differences they find in one another.

INCOMPLETE WITHOUT ONE ANOTHER

Our children have given Mike and I eight of the most extraordinary grandkids on earth. And, though it has been incredibly rewarding to watch the differences of our children emerge and grow, well, let me just say—nothing quite compares to watching the grandkids discover and embrace their differences.

Our Thanksgivings are the best now that grandchildren, niece, and nephews share a seat around our table of love. We now have two or three tables—all beautifully set for the Thanksgiving Dinner and nothing makes me happier.

Each person has different likes and dislikes on the buffet as well as in life. Any story may include a buffet of subjects—career, school, friends, current location, last great experiences, and more—rarely without laughter!

As I look around the table, I am reminded of the *Hope* I have for all of them. I personally hope for goodness and kindness in their lives. I hope for their minds to remain keen, smart, and intact forever. I hope that each understands how important it is to learn something new each day and to take every opportunity that comes their way to enrich and improve their lives. *I truly hope* each person in our family realizes the real value in the personal relationship we have with each other, because *we are so incomplete without one another.*

Gathering the family around our table always restores my faith. But, O my, does it also make me miss the people that until recently filled some very important chairs—my mother, father, brother, mother-in-law, father-in-law, and sister-in-law—they have all left this world and we feel their absence. So, though I will most certainly wipe away some tears for those absent from the table, I lift my head in gratefulness for the smiles that I still see and the sweet laughter that I hear in the conversations of our children: Mike Jr., Tammy, Mark, Deborah, and Avery. Our grown children are wonderful— three of whom, along with Dawn, Kyle, and Lyndalin, gave us *the greatest grandchildren in the world—the team of expert contributors on our family life and co-authors who are the real stars of this book.*

OUR BEAUTIFUL DIFFERENCES 2.0

I would be remiss if I failed to share with you what my grandkids bring to our table of love. *Their differences are beautiful* and have made us *more complete than we could have imagined.*

I once heard *Pastor Ed Young*, as he addressed the congregation on Grandparents Day say:

"You are Grand Parents; the title is outstanding and considered to be a step higher
than that of the child's parents. You, as a grandparent take on the role of mediator,

confidante, and most trusted friend. It is a task filled with love, light moments of laughter, and another chance to relive the good old days of childhood."

Brooke was the first grandchild—how we all waited for her with such great anticipation! The emotion I felt in becoming a grandparent was over the top! "GRANDparent"—is that *not* the grandest title ever? I never knew such joy could come from *my* children *in* their children. So, it was with great honor and joy that I held Brooke Taylor as my first grandchild. She is *strong and independent* in many ways. She has overcome many hurdles and is becoming a truly beautiful and confident woman—outspoken and loyal to defend the ones she loves. Brooke and I agree: worry is a total waste of time. All it does is steal your joy and keeps you busy doing nothing.

"*Do not worry about anything, instead, pray about everything. Tell God what you need and thank Him for all He has done.*" (Phil. 4:6-8 NLT)

Keaton came into this world looking to the left then to the right while holding his head high. I know because I had the honor to be in the room the moment he was born. No one including the doctor encouraged Keaton to arrive early. He chose *his own time in his own way.* As he has become a young man, this still applies. He is his own person with deep thoughts and beliefs that far surpass my thinking ability. Keaton's *ability to learn and retain* is a privilege that comes to few people. In a discussion once about "Nature vs. Nurture", he said to me "Genetics is the gift that just keeps on giving." His goal is to leave you with a smile on your face—seriously!

"*For this very reason, make every effort to add to your faith goodness; and to goodness, knowledge.*" (2 Pet. 1:5 NIV)

<u>Allison</u> came into the world *smiling* almost immediately and she has never stopped. Alli shares the birthday of my precious Grandmother Ann Baker who lived to be 97. She had a childhood that gave her a powerful *straight arrow approach* to life. She is *not afraid* to love you *enough* to tell you the truth. She wants *everything* to *turn out right* for you. *Be wise. Follow the rules. Stay on the straight and narrow path* while *enjoying* everything life has to offer. *Charismatic and joyful* are the words that come to mind when I think of Alli.

"God *is in her; she will not fail."* (Ps. 46:5 NIV)

<u>Grayson</u> was born on Kentucky Derby Day, and he *runs his race with a steady swiftness.* He knows what is *not* going to work in life, so he simply *applies what is going to work.* He believes *the only thing you can change is you* and, in response your environment changes. He especially enjoys getting to know people to find out what makes them tick! Grayson wants you to learn from the past: forgive, have no regrets, be genuine, and grow...

"And we know that in all things God works for the good of those who love Him, who have been called according to His purpose." (Rom. 8:28 NIV)

<u>Brittany</u> was born to ride—her hair blowing in the wind and smiling as the sun brightens her face. She feels the joy only a horse can provide. Her *shy but beautiful demeanor* comes alive when she speaks the truth about words: "You will continue to suffer, if you react to everything that is said to you." And so, she took a step back and observed with wisdom that true power is patience; that if you allow words to control you, you will always be controlled. Her confidence is growing daily.

"For we all stumble in many ways. And if anyone does not stumble in what he says, he is a perfect man, able also to bridle his whole body.

If we put bits into the mouths of horses so that they obey us, we guide their whole bodies as well." (James 3:2-3 ESV)

<u>Ciera</u> is regaining power in her life, becoming healthy and strong both mentally and physically while learning to trust God in every situation. She is leaving all fears behind her, choosing to do what she was created to do—gaining confidence in doing what is right for her. In 2018, she discovered the *true spirit of love and compassion* while teaching in a school in Kenya. Her story made a difference to all who heard her. The lives Cierra has touched will forever be ingrained in the forefront of her thinking.

"Trust in the Lord with all your heart and lean not on your own understanding; in all your ways submit to Him, and He will make your paths straight." (Prov. 3:5-6 NIV)

<u>Trevor</u> is amazingly persistent. If he fails at first, he tries again. If for some reason he does not succeed the second time, he tries yet again. *This is what I truly love about Trevor, he never stops trying.* He plugs along, not always one foot in front of the other, but he gets to the finish line just the same. *Successful* people do not give up *until* they succeed. He is shy and quiet, witty and determined. He is *sensitive and overflowing with kindness* which he truly gets from his father.

"They will soar on wings like eagles: they will run and not grow weary. They will walk and not be faint." (Isa. 40:31 NIV)

<u>Jake</u>. I believe the firstborn grandchild and lastborn grandchild are treated similarly—either they experience an abundance of everything or are slighted unintentionally in somethings. After having the first seven grandchildren, what I rooted for most, was that the family with two beautiful daughters would have the boy they so desperately wanted. Once Jake arrived, the family was completely overjoyed. Like his dad, he has tried and played almost every

sport. I have seen Jake race down slopes on skis and snowboards; proudly watched him in football, basketball, and baseball games—Jake *persevered and exceled* in them all. It appears that golf has won his heart which makes his legendary golfer grandfather very proud. Jake, *unlike* most of us, is reserved and often shy. But, without a doubt *like* the rest of us, he believes in the tradition of Family First.

"For I know the plans I have for you, declares the Lord, plans to prosper you and not to harm you, plans to give you hope and a future." (Jer. 29:11 NIV)

YOUR DIFFERENCES ARE NEEDED

Each one of the grandkids has a fierce sense of *loyalty* when it comes to family and the dynamic of family relationships. They would *all* stand up for each other in *any* situation. However, when they have a difference of opinion or think something is not correct, they are going to let it be known. *No holding back* with these young people, just *as it should be*. They *have learned early* to notice differences and *have grown* to appreciate those differences in one another.

Now, I am not saying we have all this down pat. *We are all still works in progress.* But I am saying we are learning everyday how to appreciate and embrace our differences. Not long ago, one of my granddaughters and I had a misunderstanding. It broke her heart and it broke mine too. But I must brag on that granddaughter because she was gracious enough to hear me out and, in doing so, both of our hearts were mended, and all was made right.

The problem is that many people fail to recognize that *we need these differences*. So, people say (subtly and not so subtly, with words and actions) things like, "you just need to be more like me." I would say, "If I am like you, then I do not bring anything of value to the table that is not already there. If I am like you and you are like me, then one of us is unnecessary."

Therefore, not appreciating our differences is rather silly and potentially destructive. It would be like "If all football players played defense, who would play offense? If all players were quarterbacks, who would block and who would hike the ball? If all were punt kickers, then *who would play the glorious game* of football?"

To *not* appreciate our differences does *not* work. And yet, when dysfunction raises its ugly head because it can and might, should we try to control the environment by making an effort to cause everybody to think, feel, say, and do the same? Grayson aced this question: "No, *the only thing you can change is you* and in response the environment around you changes." Sometimes that change in you is first to *value your uniqueness,* so that you can *appreciate the differences in others.*

We are a FIGHT FOR FAMILY work in progress, together winning *one battle at a time!*

Defeating Generational Dysfunction, Finding Generational Freedom

Three Empowering Principles with Three Equipping Questions to Fight FOR YOUR FAMILY

CHAPTER TEN

Principle One. We are each important because we were created to be.

Scripture: Romans 12:3 (MSG) "I'm speaking to you out of deep gratitude for all that God has given me, and especially as I have responsibilities in relation to you. Living then, as every one of you does, in pure grace, it is important that you not misinterpret yourselves as people who are bringing this goodness to God. No, God brings it all to you. The only accurate way to understand ourselves is by what God is and by what He does for us, not by what we are and what we do for Him."

Explanation: God wants us to know that we were important enough in His plan to purchase our lives with the blood of Christ. Yet, it was not because we made ourselves important. He made us, each of us, equally important. God has done and is doing and will do more for us and through us. The pressure is not on us to produce. The power is within us to produce the life we were uniquely created to live. We are important because He is making the difference in us and through us.

Question 1.

No one thinks more about you and of you than God does. Why does that matter to you?

Question 2.

What affect will this have on how you see yourself and others, when you see what God sees?

Question 3.

How will your relationships be changed when you get a firm grasp on this reality?

Principle Two.   We exist because God decided. We persist because we decide.

Scripture: 1 Corinthians 12:4, 6, 11 (NLT) "There are different kinds of spiritual gifts, but the same Spirit is the source of them all. ... God works in different ways, but it is the same God who does the work in all of us. ... It is the one and only Spirit Who distributes all these gifts. He alone decides which gift each person should have."

Explanation: The temptation to give up in relationships appears over and over again because people just want what they want from us. Their decisions did not create or orchestrate who we are or who we are becoming. So, our choice for a win-win will always be the same: value our God-designed uniqueness and appreciate our God-designed differences. The reality of our Creator's design cannot be altered by wishes or preferences. We work perfectly according to His design.

Question 1.

What have you discovered about yourself which raises your value of yourself, then causes you to love what you have discovered? What have you discovered about someone you love which raises your value of them, then causes you to love what you have discovered?

Question 2.

Do you share your appreciation of their value in your life or keep it to yourself? Why?

Question 3.

How can you encourage others to love God more by valuing yourself and appreciating them?

Principle Three.

Scripture: 1 Corinthians 12:18, 21-22, 25b-26 (NLT) "...our bodies have many parts, and God has put each part just where He wants it. ... The eye can never say to the hand, "I don't need you." The head can't say to the feet, "I don't need you." ... all the members care for each other. If one part suffers, all the parts suffer with it, and if one part is honored, all the parts are glad."

Explanation: Despite the influence of science fiction, we cannot make something be what it is not. A heart cannot be a foot, an eye cannot be a liver. A duck cannot be an eagle. We are designed to need each other. Everyone is most effective when we care for each other, not carry one another. What is truly good for one is designed to be good for all. Resist attempts to alter that reality. Fantasy hurts everyone. Working and living in God's design is amazing and satisfying.

Question 1.

Comparison and contrast are valuable when we are looking for what is best in one another. Based on reality, what do you personally bring to your relationships that no one else can?

Question 2.

How can you demonstrate that you appreciate the differences in others?

Question 3.

What do you most need from others? And what are you most glad to give to them?

Chapter Eleven
SHARE RIGHTS, RESPONSIBILITIES, AND REASONS

You must take and hold onto the highest ground of *Reasons* to win the battles of dysfunction.

We are hard-wired for love—to *receive* love and to *give* love. There is not a soul on earth that enjoys rejection in any form, shape, or size. However, no one is perfect. We have all made mistakes and felt the sting of disappointment with our own actions and with the actions of others. But this is what I have come to know down deep in my bones: It is only when *I operate out of love that I am free to be authentically me,* regardless of whether others respond in kind or not.

I now understand this is an easier thing to be said than done. Because we live in a culture which bombards us with dysfunction daily, *the truth is we must fight to learn how to operate in the fullest measure of confidence which is found only in being authentically who we are created to be.* Even though we are fully known and thoroughly loved by God, we still stumble at times into a destructive game of comparison because none of us wants to be excluded, rejected, or measured and found wanting. Yet, there are those moments when we *second guess* ourselves and miss the opportunity to operate out of our truest sense of who He has created each of us to be.

COULD, SHOULD, AND WOULD

Impacted by dysfunction, this is how things often play out in our lives. We think about all the things that have happened over the course of our lifetime. Then, out of the blue, someone asks those dreaded questions: "Would you have changed any of the things that you have done? If you could have, would you have done things differently? Would you have altered this or that? Would you not have done certain things or done other things instead? Would you replace any decision with another? And before we know it, doubt moves in and we begin to measure our efforts against all the *"could have, should have, and would have"* the world can toss at us.

Doubt is a *battlefield* set for *ambush.* Guilt, whether groundless or earned, gives your opponent the advantage. People will gladly fight for their *rights* to weigh you down with guilt-ridden *responsibility* without legitimate *reason,* just to hold the advantage of higher ground.

I know! It is awful! But if we are honest, everyone one of us has battled our regrets and they are a terrible measuring rod for assessing our value and our worth. However, because at some point in our lives we will battle them, I would like to offer another perspective, because there is some wisdom to be gained in hindsight.

You see, I understand that I could have done a lot of things because I had a right to do a lot of things. I had a right to do a lot of things because I was a daughter, a sister, a wife, a mother, an aunt, a grandmother, a friend, and a boss. *Those roles gave me certain rights.* But I did not use them. In many circumstances, I wished I had done a lot of things. Yet in other circumstances where I did not, I am glad that I did not exercise my right.

Stay with me on this. Please keep reading because I am going somewhere with all of this.

Looking back, this is what I know: I should have done a good many things—not just because *it was my right*, but because *it was also my responsibility* in any one of those given roles. I should have exercised my responsibility because I was daughter, a sister, a wife, a mother, an aunt, a grandmother, a friend, and a boss. Thankfully, *in most cases I did* what I could, should, and would. Sometimes people it took it well and sometimes people did not.

There were times when I should have done or said something, and I did not—*we all can say that about ourselves.* Without question, people still remember those times, and some choose never to forget. No matter what our relationship might be or might have been, we all deeply regret those things—because it was our responsibility.

A QUESTION WORTH PONDERING

However, because we cannot go back and do it all over again, here is what I want to say to you: Today, if I had to do those things all over again, the most important question I would ask myself is the *would I have* question—not the *could I have* or *should I have* question because so much of life is *wasted* on those two questions.

What would I have done differently, knowing what I know now?

That is the question from which we can grow leaps and bounds. Like, "Would I have kept my mouth shut, when my emotions and my ego cried for defense?" I would. "Would I have *taken the next right step,* even when I was afraid?" I would—I would have been braver. More examples remain for me. And what about you, my friend? Are there things that you would have done differently *if your heart and soul were spurring you onward and upward?*

The questions that address our "would we"—*the questions of our will*—are worth pondering because, without a doubt, I know there are those things that all of us would have said and done differently because we want better for ourselves and for those our lives influence forever. If we were given another chance, we would want to do better and would.

You know what I mean—like those times when a couple of minutes or even a couple of seconds later, we wished we would have *said it differently,* wished we would have *left out one word,* wished we would have *spoken with a different tone of voice,* wished we would have *spoken the truth in love* simply because *we were motivated to love like Jesus.*

WHAT WOULD JESUS DO?

Just imagine for a moment being with Jesus, walking with him from village to village, and observing the many times that He could have done *anything that He wanted to do* if He wanted to because He was Jesus—fully God and fully man. Because He was the Son of God, *He had the right to do anything.* He could have called down thousands of angels on His behalf. He could have feasted instead of fasted in the wilderness. He could have thrown stones at the woman caught in the very act of adultery instead of stooping low to write in the sand. O, the things He could have done *if He wanted to.* But *Love has a reason* that supersedes your rights and your responsibilities.

Betrayed by Peter, Jesus should never have entrusted His church to Peter's care. When Paul persecuted His church, Jesus should never have made Paul His spokesman. And when Thomas doubted the resurrection, Jesus should never have had to extend His nail scarred hands as proof to that doubting disciple. But Love has a reason that *surpasses your rights and your responsibilities.*

Recently, a friend pointed out to me that the first recorded words of Jesus are *"Did you not know that I must be about my Father's business?"*[29] Even though He was the Son of God and could have said or done whatever He wanted, Jesus understood from the very beginning of time that *"love does not force its rightful claim"*[30] but chooses joyfully to fulfill the will of the Father. Jesus was sent by God to communicate His Father's love for a lost and dying world. Jesus' whole mission was to reveal His Father's heart so that fallen humanity could be redeemed and restored to perfect relationship with His Father. Therefore, though He possessed the right to do anything, because He was the Son of God, He would not do anything except what He saw His Father doing in the lives of each person He met.

By interacting with people that way, Jesus demonstrated that, though we may at times be entitled to rights and responsibilities, *it is only when love directs our course of action* that *we have a reason to speak the truth.* Indeed, like Jesus, as human beings, we are endowed with certain rights and responsibilities. Yet simultaneously, *we were created first and foremost to represent our Father.* Created in His image, we carry and show His image to the world. All our *"could haves, should haves, and would haves"* are to be motivated *by reason of His love for those around us.* We choose not to love like the world loves, warm and fuzzy but often with no substance. Instead, we choose love that reveals our Father's Heart to all the world—*a love that seeks the highest good of others...even on hard days.*

BEYOND RIGHTS AND RESPONSIBILITES

Who among us has not had those moments where our regrets threaten to undo us? But now that I am "feeling the seasons," meaning I have lived long enough to have gained some wisdom, I have reached a noteworthy conclusion. It is not that we should never ask the questions of regret, (because that would be impossible) but rather, *in those moments,* we should ask *this question* "Would I have done differently, if I knew then what I know *now?*" Why is this *would have* question so important? Because *similar situations are likely to appear in our lives and in the lives of those we love. This would have question* provides us with an insightful tool for better future choices and outcomes.

For example: In the heat of the moment, when things are hard and the pressure is on, think through what is happening and ask, "Do I have a *right?* More times than not, the answer will probably be, "Yes, I have a right." Then ask, "Do I have a *responsibility?*" And the answer will also probably be, "Yes, I have a responsibility." But even more important than having the right and the responsibility to act and respond accordingly is to ask ourselves a final question—"Do I have a *reason?*" And if the answer is "Yes, I have a reason" take it one step further and ask, "But is it *a Jesus reason?*" Stop to ask yourself honestly "Am I operating in response to this situation out of a *motive of love?*" If the answer is yes—THAT, my friend, is a *GAME CHANGER.*

When we make the decision that out of *a motive of love* we will do what we could have, should have, and would have—not for our reputation's sake or because we do not want to be criticized—but because we are determined to be motivated to act, speak, and be as our Father would—*THAT is when we truly begin to live authentically!*

COMPELLED BY LOVE

Love is the only reason that should compel any of us to act, speak and be. If Jesus was unwavering in His determination to only do what He saw His Father doing, we should strive to let the same love that Jesus had for His Father be the reason that governs all our acting, speaking, and being. A love that compels us to speak, act, or be is a love that is not looking for reciprocation. It is a love that has moved beyond childish and selfish ways.

In the Passion Translation, 1st Corinthians 13:4-8a, and 11 sums all this up when it says:

"Love is large and incredibly patient. Love is gentle and consistently kind to all. It refuses to be jealous when blessing comes to someone else. Love does not brag about one's achievements nor inflate its own importance. Love does not traffic in shame and disrespect, nor selfishly seek its own honor. Love is not easily irritated or quick to take offense. Love joyfully celebrates honesty and finds no delight in what is wrong. Love is a safe place of shelter, for it never stops believing the best for others. Love never takes failure as defeat, for it never gives up. Love never stops loving. ... When I was a child, I spoke about childish matters, for I saw things like a child and reasoned like a child. But the day came when I matured, and I set aside my childish ways."

If we remain childish or selfish in our ways, we will not *respond from a place of love* but rather *react from a place of dysfunction*. But, if we are compelled by love to put our childish and selfish ways behind us, we will begin to mature with a love that grows stronger every day.

We all grow *older*, but we do not all grow *up*. Some of us grow up to have great conversations and share amazing opportunities with the people that we know and love. Some of those conversations catch us by surprise and provide deep insight into the maturing minds and hearts of others. That is exactly what happened in a recent conversation with my grandson Grayson. He told the story of discovering and owning his own voice—it was *PRICELESS!*

GRAYSON

Let me try to do justice in the retelling of his story. Imagine that you are Grayson. You are in a conversation with your mother and suddenly you realize that you have an opinion that differs from hers. It feels uncomfortable because, until this moment, you have never voiced an opinion that differs from hers—maybe you had one in mind, but you were never brave enough to counter her opinion—until now. But, O my, you can no longer hold your tongue, and for the first time ever you find yourself saying: "Hold on a minute, *I do not agree.*"

That is what happened to Grayson. He had an opinion that started all the way down in the tips of his toes, came all the way up through his throat, and spilled straight out of his mouth. Before he could even think about "could I, should I, would I", it landed all over his mother. It was then that he consulted with himself: "Oops, did I have a right to say that?" In his heart, he already knew that he indeed had a right to hold his own opinion because he was a human being too. His mother had taught him well. And, he had a right to his opinion, even if it disagreed with hers.

Standing there in those couple of seconds which seemed like an eternity, he thought "O my goodness, she is my mother and I am her son, and I care about her. She needs to *know* what I think because what if sharing my opinion *stops* her from making a mistake—a mistake that I think could lead to great *heartbreak* for her? What if what I have to say really *matters*? What if what I say helps her to make the *right* choice?"

He knew in that moment he had a *responsibility* to say what others could not always say because he had carried the role of confidant ever since he was a small boy when the family split in two. His mother found it easy to share her hopes, dreams, and heartaches with Grayson because he seemed to be the one that best *understood* her world. He knew on that day that, if he did not share his differing opinion with her, no one else *would*. It was a moment of *truth*; a moment of *maturity*. He had *a right and a responsibility* to share his opinion—but mostly he had *a reason* to share his differing opinion with her *because love compelled him*. Her life now is not the same as it might have been had he *not* loved her enough to speak truth.

I am sure Grayson has had days where he wonders: What *would* have happened had he not shared his concern for her? What *would* have happened had he not stepped up? What *would* have happened had he not risen to the occasion and acted in a responsible but loving way?

Watching Grayson move from *childhood into manhood* has been like watching a sudden rainstorm appear on the horizon out of nowhere, glorious in its wonder and power to cause change. In finding his voice, *Gray* discovered that it was not *just* his right or *just* his responsibility to share his opinions with his mother, but it was *more his reason—his love for his mother* that compelled him to speak the truth...even when *opinions* differ.

If you asked him today, "Why did you say what you said?" He would *share* his "Why" *freely* in typical Grayson *style*—It was neither his right nor his responsibility that compelled him; *it was his reason* that gave him courage to do what was no less than what she deserved—his best, that it was what she knew she could count on from him—and that, as usual, his love for her is what she always received from him, challenging or not!

Truth, when spoken in love, sets people free!

When Grayson settled the issue of rights, responsibilities, and reasons, he began to walk in the truth of 1st Corinthians 13:11. *"When I was a child, I spoke about childish matters, for I saw things like a child and reasoned like a child. But the day came when I matured, and I set aside my childish ways."31*

I cannot help but think that watching my grandchildren grow up and mature in love for God and others goes back to that photo *I received from my brother—the photo of his newborn only grandson.* When I looked at that photo of Drake—I knew in an instant—*I had a right, a responsibility, and a reason* to *gather* my grandchildren around the table of love and *invite* them to *identify* potential obstacles and *develop* a strategy for overcoming life's challenges.

It is because I loved my parents, it is because I loved my brother, it is because I love my nephew Ty, it is because I love my husband and all our kids, it is because I love all my grandchildren, niece, and nephews, and all the people that worked for me! In *every* situation I had a right *and* I had a responsibility. But it was not until I really *learned the reason for speaking the truth and the reason for doing the right thing* that all my fears were conquered. *I know that love in word and deed is what sets people free!*

How do I know? Because *now I AM FREE!*

You see, when we choose to *act* in love without waiting for our *feelings* to come, our commitment to lasting relationship sets a legacy in motion while we are alive that still expresses itself and grows long after we are gone!

LOVE is the right *reason* and *motive* that guarantees that *your legacy will touch the world!*

Defeating Generational Dysfunction, Finding Generational Freedom
Three Empowering Principles with Three Equipping Questions to Fight FOR YOUR FAMILY

CHAPTER ELEVEN

Principle One. We give rights to ensure that "what is right" is a shared experience.

Scripture: 1 Corinthians 9:12 (MSG) "Others demand plenty from you in these ways. Don't we who have never demanded deserve even more? But we're not going to start demanding now what we've always had a perfect right to. "

Explanation: Rights are based on reciprocation (which is appreciated, desirable, and enforceable by law to its extent). Healthy satisfying relationships cannot be based on reciprocation. "If I have to" you are not satisfied; you are appeased. So, to drop our demands is a sign that we understand how relationships work, grow, and flourish. You and I do gain understanding from our rights when we know, trust, and do God's law. Loving Him, ourselves, and others summarizes His law.

Question 1.

What does "having rights" mean to you? How do you value the rights of others?

Question 2.

How effective are you in offering and expecting "rights"? Do you know when to use them?

Question 3.

If, as Paul wrote, "we are not going to start demanding", then what should our response be when others choose not to reciprocate?

Principle Two. We choose responsibility over rights in relationships...wisely.

Scripture: Galatians 4:5-7 (MSG) "...we have been set free to experience our rightful heritage. You can tell for sure that you are now fully adopted as His own children because God sent the Spirit of His Son into our lives crying out, "Papa! Father!" Doesn't that privilege of intimate conversation with God make it plain that you are not a slave, but a child? And if you are a child, you're also an heir, with complete access to the inheritance."

Explanation: There is no question that rights are valuable. More than rights, responsibility characterizes the foundation of family relationships. Love is what drives responsibility. God did not just speak about it. He demonstrated it from Day One of creation and sacrificed the blood of His Son to responsibly buy back the relationship with us that He created. God can expect us to respond to Him responsibly because He is our Father, we are His and He is ours.

Question 1.

Responsibility is not about entitlement, although our world wants to change responsibility's meaning and intention. How does embracing responsibility for yourself and for your part in anything make a difference in your world?

Question 2.

How is responsibility a two-way street that you walk gladly because of your commitment to lasting relationship with others?

Question 3.

What are you willing to do instead of demanding what you are entitled to? What are you willing to forfeit to show that you hold yourself responsible? Why is your example so necessary?

Principle Three. We have reasons that motivate us to grow up, step up, and go up.

Scripture: Ephesians 4:15-16 (MSG) "God wants us to grow up, to know the whole truth and tell it in love—like Christ in everything. We take our lead from Christ, Who is the source of everything we do. 16 He keeps us in step with each other. His very breath and blood flow through us, nourishing us so that we will grow up healthy in God, robust in love."

Explanation: God loves you just as you are. As His child, He calls you to grow up, step up, and go up. A loving Father teaches us through the discipline and suffering of obedience what matters most in relationships. Without obedience, Jesus would never have died on your cross. *Reasons* keep details of the bigger picture in mind. Following the leadership of the Lord Jesus, we have reasons to take one another's health and growth seriously. We rise to the occasion's life presents to us.

Question 1.

Where do you need to grow up? What steps will you take today?

Question 2.

Where do you need to step up? What have you let go too far, where you have not acted on reasons?

Question 3.

Where do you need to go that is higher than "what is now too familiar" and is beneath your potential?

Chapter Twelve
BE LOYAL, DISEMPOWER CODEPENDENCY

I f you knew me or any part of my story, then you would know *there is a story* that some people who know me expect me to tell—a not so pretty story, a war story.

This story started for me when I was a child. Your story began to unfold in childhood as it does for all of us. You and I have an enemy—so with every broken promise, with every unfulfilled expectation, he whispers his lies: you cannot depend on people ever, you cannot even depend on God. This is the common story human beings buy into at an age far too young. I did.

I will be the first to admit that my life has not been a walk in the park. It has been peppered with heartache, a few shattered dreams, and the brokenness of dysfunction. But if I were to tell *that story only*, I would be telling THE COMMON STORY: the one that some people expect to hear, the one that some people swear is the truth, the one that some people have only ever seen through human eyes. To be sure, it would be a story tainted and stained with the dirt of this world. *That is the story some people think you and I should tell.*

But what good would that do? Because to tell the Common Story is to offer up a story without *hope*, without *redemption*, without *forgiveness* and without *power*. The Common Story is a story based on *facts without mercy, facts without grace.* And I will *not* tell that story for it is *not* my story.

THE COMMON STORY

The sad truth of the matter, one that I have observed far too many times, is that the Common Story is rarely a spoken one because of what the world deems as *Loyalty*—albeit a false loyalty at that.

For example, you have probably heard on more than one occasion the familiar admonishment, "If you cannot say anything good, do not say anything at all." Under normal healthy circumstances, that would be great advice—advice that should be followed. But, throw a good dose of unhealthy co-dependency into the mix of a dysfunctional family and what comes out of the mouth often sounds like one of these sentences: "You better not say anything, or you will be sorry. You better not speak about this or something might happen, something bad that is! You better not or there will be heck to pay. You better not or you will never hear the end of it. You better not say anything—especially do not tell the truth—because people will not understand, and you will ruin everything."

Well, that kind of loyalty is <u>not</u> *Loyalty* at all—it is *detrimental*, it is *codependency*, and it is *manipulation* at its worst. That kind of loyalty is *fabricated* on keeping up appearances, on image, on masks, on one-hand-washes-the-other, and on you-owe-me-one. That kind of loyalty must weigh its words very carefully and be willing to set the TRUTH aside, and maybe even *lie* in a limited or full-blown way, if necessary. That kind of loyalty is *rotten* at its core, eventually its *proof* reaches the surface.

That kind of loyalty sets itself up as *more important* than Love and Truth because it is always *more concerned with one's personal reputation* than the good of others or the good of the family. That kind of loyalty thinks only of *itself* and has little interest in the perspective of others. *A win-win scenario* is not even on the table for those caught in *the crossfires of generational dysfunction.* Unfortunately, the Common Story is perpetrated in a million little ways in millions of homes every single day. That kind of loyalty is *destroying people's lives.*

PAST TRANSGRESSIONS

I would venture to say all this because *the dysfunction of codependency and manipulation* tends to be *multigenerational.* At one time or another, most of us have been immobilized by co-dependency, broken and trashed by manipulation (either observed or experienced) whether *intended or unintended.*

We have seen it up close and personal. It has left us with deep wounds and intense longing for healing, wholeness, peace, and joy to be present within our hearts and our homes. We know the suffering and the sorrow that dysfunctional behavior leaves in its wake and we cannot help but wonder, "Will the ones that have caused hurt ever humble themselves and ask for forgiveness? And, if *offenders* ever do come to their senses and seek forgiveness, will those that have been *wounded* forgive the offender?" *Mercy and grace come from God,* but it is *extended through us.* Oh, that we ourselves would choose to be free from the Common Story.

The questions that determine the *quality* of our story are "How do we FIGHT *FOR* our families with our families, and not FIGHT *AGAINST* our families with or without allies? How do we end the COMMON STORY, stop the damage, and heal the hurt?"

First, we need to acknowledge that to be part of a family means that we have all played a role in how we got from there to here and why we are stuck.

Second, for change to come so that there can be a better life for everyone, we must each *acknowledge* the past and all its mistakes, *seek* true forgiveness, and then we must *not allow ourselves to stay fixated on the PAST.*

To try and fix the past is an *insatiable* process—it is never *satisfyable* and never *satisfactory.* But, to move forward, it is necessary that we ask the forgiveness of our past wrongs, so that our present and future can be embraced, and that we might live life to the fullest. Because in truth, we have *all* done wrong and have *all* been wronged.

Third, we have lived as givers, survived as takers, and struggled as receivers. We have longed to be loved and have avoided getting close to others. We have called into question the motives and sincerity of others, yet demanded to be indisputably trusted, believed and respected ourselves. Can we not see that *we all stand in need of much mercy and much grace?* Therefore, it would greatly benefit us to forgive *ourselves* and *one another* for our past offenses.

UNMET EXPECTATIONS

So *why* do we find it so difficult to leave the Common Story behind? I think it has something to do with *unmet expectations.* Given the fact that I have lived seven decades, I have watched *the unfolding of unmet expectations time and time again and it never ends well.*

Let me explain. Two people enter a relationship: it could be a husband and wife, a girlfriend and boyfriend, a father and a son, a mother and a daughter, two friends, two siblings, two co-workers, an employer and an employee. Simply, it is two people in some type of a relationship; one has an expectation—a longing, a desire, a hope, but the other doesn't know anything about that expectation, because it's never been an expressed expectation.

Imagine if you will that there is a lovely young bride who adores fresh flowers. As a little girl, she grew up watching her daddy waltz into the kitchen every Friday night with a bouquet of flowers for her sweet mother who was standing at the kitchen stove making supper for her husband and her children. Now, in that young bride's mind, nothing says "I love you!" like a man bringing home flowers on a Friday night. The *only* problem is—she has never once shared with her young groom that she wants flowers just like her father gave her mother. She just assumed he would know that every girl wants flowers on a Friday night! But (clue-less) he does not know that, because (tool-less) he never saw that example when he was growing up.

Regrettably, the young husband has no idea that his new bride is disappointed and feels very much unloved. As the days and weeks turn into months, she nurses a wound he knows nothing about. And my gosh, how *unfair* it is of her to hold this disappointment against him when she has never once shared with him that "Nothing says 'I love you!' like a man bringing home flowers on a Friday night."

I know this might seem like a silly example, but let me just say this, *more marriages have fallen apart because of unmet expectations. Business partnerships have fallen apart because of unmet expectations. Friendships have fallen apart because of unmet expectations. Families have fallen apart because of unmet expectations.*

Within my own family, there have been times that we have disappointed one another because of unmet expectations. We made *assumptions* about one another and *assumed* things that may or may not have even been true. We *unwittingly harbored* unmet expectations (for years) because we *incorrectly assumed* that the other person should just *know* how we feel, should just *know* what we want, should just *know* what is in our mind and in our heart...*even though we never expressed those expectations to one another.* Seriously, how ridiculous can that be? I *know* you know...

CHOOSE FORGIVENESS, ROUT DYSFUNCTION

Unmet *expectations* always give way to *disappointment.* And *disappointment* gives way to *distance* being created between people who at one time or another thought each other hung the moon.

The other day, my granddaughter Brooke, who is our oldest grandchild and the one who has had the longest running *front row seat* to "The Willis Story," had an opportunity to reflect on a bit of our history with my editing team. In spite of all the ups and downs and the high and lows she has witnessed, her insight was profound, her words compellingly beautiful (and I dare say possibly prophetic) because I think *her words hold the key to breaking free from the Common Story* that seeks to hold every one of us captive.

Brooke said in retrospect: "If I could share anything with my family, I would say, 'There is *nothing* else I would rather express than to say *forgiveness is one of the most powerful choices that we have.* So, I hope that *everyone* chooses to use it. Or else, people will just sit there *stuck* with their disappointment. So, if *you* are disappointed, *you* have the choice to forgive the person for their shortcoming that *you* experienced which did not meet *your* expectation. All I really would hope for my family is that *we would all learn* to forgive because things in life are clearly going to keep happening and mistakes are clearly going to keep getting made. *It is so important to forgive.*"

Is that not *simply powerful?* I know I am her grandmother and I think she is *amazing!* But those are still *profoundly wise* words.

CHOOSE FORGIVENESS, ROUT DYSFUNCTION! *Rout* it out, beat it, defeat it, overthrow it, crush it hard, smash it down, send it sprinting back from whence it came!

To receive forgiveness and to extend forgiveness is the key to leaving the Common Story behind. Do you not see and understand that *we do not need one more* Common Story? We are drowning in a sea of common stories that play out before our eyes every single day. Another broken promise, another shattered dream, another failure, another rejection, another disappointment—the common stories just suck the life right out of us.

DECLARE WAR AGAINST THE COMMON STORY

What we need is an UNCOMMON STORY. What you need is an UNCOMMON STORY. What families all over the world need is an UNCOMMON STORY!

I wrote this book to *declare war against the common story—* because the common story is *not* the story that *God has written for us or for our families.* Psalm 139:16-17 teaches each of us to definitively declare "You [God] saw who You created me to be before I became me! Before I'd ever seen the light of day, the number of days You planned for me were already recorded in Your book. Every single moment You were thinking of me!"[32]

God has written AN UNCOMMON STORY for each of us.

I wrote this book with my grandchildren so that my family, your family, and every future generation might know there is AN UNCOMMON STORY waiting to be told through our lives. *My story is AN UNCOMMON STORY* and *I hope your story will be too!*

You must understand that we have *an unseen enemy* who has been around since the dawn of time. He does not want you to *leave* the Common Story *behind* and *embrace* the UNCOMMON STORY that *God has written for you. Our enemy has one agenda and one agenda only*—to convince the world that the only story that exists for mankind is the common story. He wants you to believe that only what you can see with your human eyes, only what you can hear with your human ears, and only what you can feel with your broken heart...is all that will ever be. That is the story he wants you to believe. That is The Common Story and it is *not* THE TRUTH.

Because you see, what is impossible for us—impossible for our family—is possible with God! Without God, as our *ally*, we face a fight we cannot win. *But, with Almighty God, as our ally, we face a fight He has promised us to win. In fact, the victory is His and the battle has already been won on our behalf!*

James 4:7-10 clearly shows us the way to defeat our enemy. Listen. It will be good for your soul, I promise. "So, let God work His will in you. *Yell a loud no to the Devil* and watch him scamper. *Say a quiet yes to God* and he'll be there in no time. Quit dabbling in sin. Purify your inner life. Quit playing the field. Hit bottom and cry your eyes out. The fun and games are over. Get serious, very serious. Get down on your knees before the Master; it's the only way you'll get on your feet." If that isn't enough encouragement for you, God has also promised "to give you a new heart, put a new spirit within you ... to remove the stony heart from your body and replace it with a heart that's God-willed, not self-willed."[33]

God is FOR YOU....He is NOT AGAINST YOU. (Romans 8:31 *paraphrase mine*)

EMBRACE THE UNCOMMON STORY

To my sweet family I say: "When you look at us, I know you see our messes. There may be times you may not believe in one another, but I believe in you always because God believes in you. This is the lesson *I have been learning my whole life long*—the lesson that is *my legacy to you.*

To leave the Common Story behind and embrace the UNCOMMON STORY written for you long before you were born *will be a <u>battle</u>.* But *it is a WAR that you can win* when you choose to believe that things are not always as they appear because *the common story is not the real story. The real story,* the truest story you will ever know, *is found when you embrace the UNCOMMON STORY.*

In the best war stories, people always describe how tough the *battle* truly was, how sweet the *victory* truly became, and how loved the *heroes* were to all who shared each battle. *We are the kind of family we choose to be. We are each able to become the heroes we were created to be! To choose God's UNCOMMON STORY is a choice to WIN TOGETHER!*

Just remember, people do not always do what they *want* to do. They often do what is *comfortable,* what feels *possible,* what is *familiar,* what they have *always done,* and what has *always resulted* in falling into the same old trap that we have seen for generations.

But *the time has come* to FIGHT FOR *Our* FAMILY—to *defeat generational dysfunction and to find generational freedom!* Things will *not* be as they have *always been so far, unless we choose to leave them that way.* I pray for *each* of you that you will *embrace AN UNCOMMON STORY and walk the better road!*

I am *learning* to *LOVE* to tell my story! I have told all you need to know about *my old story*, while we have been telling *our new story*. And, *we want YOU to have A NEW STORY*—or we would not have invested ourselves into this book *for YOU!*

Defeating Generational Dysfunction, Finding Generational Freedom

Three Empowering Principles with Three Equipping Questions to Fight FOR YOUR FAMILY

CHAPTER TWELVE

Principle One. We can count on God to be loyal.

Scripture: Psalm 147:3 (NLT) "He heals the brokenhearted and bandages their wounds."

Explanation: In the military, there is a saying "Leave no man behind". In the Bible, lost sheep are valuable enough to search for, find, and restore. God is unquestionably loyal and uncondemning of His own. When we agree that He is our God and we agree that we are His, He will not rest until we yield ourselves to His compassionate arms. It is there that He teaches us again His ways which are always good. He does not leave us without careful correction, direction, and strength.

Question 1.

Unmet expectations are what keeps us brokenhearted and wounded. Who is responsible for communicating a need? But Who is ultimately responsible for meeting needs?

Question 2.

God is ready for our honesty. We are safe in sharing our expectations. Are you ready for His answers to finding true loyalty?

Question 3.

What are you willing to do and say to make truly loyal character evident?

Principle Two. We experience genuine loyalty when are humble before God.

Scripture: James 4:10 (NLT) "Humble yourselves before the Lord, and He will lift you up in honor".

Explanation: God's favor is much more important than the approval of people. He demonstrates His loyalty to us when we choose to humble ourselves before Him. Others shift their loyalty to us or from us, based on their approval or disapproval of us. When we humbly seek to honor God, He gives us favor even with those who do not agree with Him or make the same choices that we make. The closer we all move toward honoring God, the more loyalty we share in Him.

Question 1.
Why is loyalty "healthy" when we humble ourselves before God?

Question 2.
How are unhealthy patterns broken when we make God central to our relationships?

Question 3.
How will you change your relationships by making loyalty to God your priority?

Principle Three. We can expect God to give us His kind of lifechanging loyalty.

Scripture: Ezekiel 36:26 (MSG) "I'll give you a new heart, put a new spirit in you. I'll remove the stone heart from your body and replace it with a heart that's God-willed, not self-willed."

Explanation: God is not hard-hearted toward our disloyalty. He has a solution for it. Instead of being hard-hearted toward us, He promises to give us a new heart and spirit. He promises to remove the hard heart and replace it, no questions asked. All He waits for is our sincere request. Our new heart and spirit will make us think, feel, act, and live in new ways. We will not be the same when we share His kind of loyalty with one another. Old ways will be gone, new life together will begin.

Question 1.

What hard-heartedness are you willing to lay down, in order to humbly receive the new heart and new spirit that true loyalty requires?

Question 2.

How will the choice you make encourage others to do the same?

Question 3.

What do you expect this kind of change will produce? With that change, what will you need next from God to keep moving forward?

Chapter Thirteen
MAKE A NEW LIFECHANGING MESSAGE OUT OF AN OLD REPRODUCING MESS

I was eleven years old. I was also of the age that I dialed a rotary phone if I made a phone call, and I listened to my 45s on my record player which was my most prized possession.

On this day, I was sitting with my precious mother on the couch watching our black and white television with tin foil on top of the rabbit ear antenna. As we often did, we were watching a Billy Graham Crusade. Mother loved his preaching. I was restless because I truly loved the music more than I ever loved the sermon and the music had just ended. Thankfully, Dr. Graham began by telling a story that grabbed my attention and his preaching quickly became much more interesting.

THE GOSSIP, THE VICAR, AND THE FEATHERS

"There is a story of a woman in England who came to her vicar with a troubled conscience." He proceeded, "The vicar knew her to be a habitual gossip who often spread bad unkind words—she had maligned nearly everyone in the village.

"Reverend Father, how can I make amends?" she pleaded. The vicar said, "If you want to make peace with your conscience, take a bag of goose feathers and drop one on the porch of each person you have slandered or of whom you have wrongly spoken."

When she had finished this task, she came back to the vicar and said, "Is that all?" "No," said the wise vicar, "now you must go and gather up each feather, then bring them back to me." After many hours, the woman returned without a single feather. "The wind has blown them all away," she said. "My dear woman," said the vicar, "so it is with unkind words or gossip; they are so easily dropped, but we can never take them back again."[34]

FIGHTIN' WORDS

After the show had ended, my precious mother looked me in the eyes and said, "There are many words I wish I had never spoken, and I wish I could take back." My mother spoke in a beautiful soft voice most of the time. However, as she proceeded to tell me a story of her childhood, she started to raise her voice …

When she was thirteen and her youngest brother was six, a group of rag tag boys (mother's description) followed them home from school in rural Kentucky. Most of the families in that area lived on farms and there was quite a distance between each farm. Mother said the boys were yelling mean things at them and called them bad names—things that only young stupid 15-year-old boys would say. Well, Mother and her brother Charlie started to walk as fast as their legs would carry them. However, Charlie slipped and fell and one of the boys threw a rock that landed square in the middle of the back of his head—it started to bleed. Mother was so afraid that she started screaming. Her father was working in the tobacco field nearby, heard the screams, and ran to help. Those spiteful rag tag boys scattered as my grandfather arrived.

They took my Uncle Charlie home and attended to his wounded head. My mother continued to tell me the story with tears glistening in her eyes. She said, "I felt so afraid for dear sweet Charlie, I was supposed to protect him, however I failed." Now, it is important to know Mother was the only girl with five brothers. She was overprotected most of her young life *by* her brothers.

That same evening, while sitting at the dinner table with three of her older brothers and young Charlie, she recounted the horror story that had happened that afternoon. Her oldest brother Howard said, "I will meet you after school tomorrow and I will walk both of you home." Mother said all her fears were over for at least twenty-four hours.

The next day after school, Mother went to Uncle Charlie's classroom to get him for the walk home. Instead of walking, they sat on the front steps of the school and waited for big brother Howard to arrive. When fifteen minutes had passed, the rag tag group of four older boys saw them sitting on the steps and came to taunt them. My mother said her heart started racing and pounding as she gripped Charlie's hand and she whispered, "Do not be afraid!"

At that point in the story, I am all ears—hanging on every word of the story my mother is telling me. All of a sudden, that sweet quiet precious mother of mine stood up from the couch and, with the biggest booming voice I had ever heard come out of her mouth, she yelled "My brother told me to tell you he is coming for us and he is bringing Hell with him!" With excitement she said, "Right about that time, our brother Howard (all six foot three of him) showed up right on Mother's cue and announced: "I'm here!" As quickly as those boys had arrived, they scattered like scalded dogs when Uncle Howard showed up. My mother said she had never been happier in her life to see her big brother.

WORDS WE REGRET

Now, the moral to this story is what my mother said next. "Dear Sweet Francie," (that is what she called me when she spoke to me in those teachable moments) "I screamed at the top of my lungs that my brother was coming and bringing Hell with him because I had once heard my own mother scream aloud to us, "tell your father I am coming to that bar to get him and I am bringing Hell with me!"

My mother never forgot those words, and she recounted often that my grandmother regretted till her dying day that she used a curse word in front of her kids. And I know that to be true, because as I grew up, Granny (as we called her) told me the story of her big outburst time and time again. My granny, Stacey Ann Baker, lived to be ninety-seven years old. She was almost blind, wore a hearing aid, but was never ill. She did not have dementia or Alzheimer's disease—she was sharp as a tack until she drew her last breath.

I was only eleven years old when my Mother told me that story. And just like Granny and Mother, who could never shake from their memories the outburst of their words, I too have never forgotten their story.

That is the *two-edged sword* of words—once spoken they can never be withdrawn. In their book, *The Power of Words and The Wonder of God,* John Piper and Justin Taylor remind us that "Words carry immeasurable significance: The universe was created with a word; Jesus healed and cast out demons with a word; rulers have risen and fallen by their words. The tongue is a powerful force—for good or for evil."[35]

Regrettably, most of us fail to *recognize and respect* the power of words. Consequently, we either spit them out with little thought of the ramifications of our words, or we fail to carefully use them altogether—therefore withholding a kindness or an affirmation that could mend a broken heart.

If you were to Google "what the Bible says about the power of our words" you would discover hundreds of books and articles have been written about the power of the tongue and that words have the power to build up or tear down. Contained within many of the writings is an underlying caution that we should choose words carefully before uttering them to another or even to ourselves.

In fact, the most important words we may ever speak *could* be the words we speak to *ourselves*—because those words have the power to instill beliefs, create our mindset, establish our self-image, and shape our worldview. Is it not conceivable even likely that when the Bible tells us to "love our neighbors as we love ourselves"[36] it indicates that we need to speak life, hope, truth, and love, not just to our neighbors but to ourselves as well? What do you speak to yourself? We need to be very mindful of our "thought words." Proverbs 23:7 tells us that "For as he [a man] thinks in his heart so he is."[37] If we correctly understood the power of our thoughts, both spoken and unspoken, we would guard our thinking like precious jewels.

PREACHING TO THE CHOIR

The apostle Paul wrote, "Do not let any unwholesome talk come out of your mouths, but only what is helpful for building others up according to their needs, that it may benefit those who listen."[38] I truly believe that to be Christ-like means we should not use rotten, corrupting language. But today, the use of filthy language is heard on every street corner and sadly, even in places of worship. People tend to think it is macho or liberating to use vulgar humor, dirty jokes, and foul language in front of younger children and even older kids. Examples like these stay with a young mind and cause great confusion as time goes on. Children are totally dependent on loved ones to bring them up. They want to emulate and be like grown-ups.

I cannot help but wonder "How have we come to this place that as parents, relatives, or siblings we would distort children's thinking with words that are harmful and hurtful?" Surely unwholesome words should not have a place in the mind or an utterance from the mouths of those of us who claim to love Jesus. It is a sad when we use horrible words in our conversations with one another and then walk into church on any given Sunday and profess with our mouths that we love the Lord and believe in God. In the light of Paul's words, "But only speak what is helpful for building others up according to their needs, that it may benefit those who listen."[39] and "Let your conversation be always full of grace, seasoned with salt, so that you may know how to answer everyone."[40]—clearly, we are missing the mark.

In case you think I am judging everyone else but myself, please know, I am preaching to the choir—asking God to help me right along with you. Oh, my goodness, I know that I am so guilty of spouting off and rushing to speak. I know I should take more time remembering that children, young and old, are hearing my words. Subsequently, because I know this, Paul's words convict my heart. He urges us to be a blessing to those with whom we have daily contact. Yet, if we are honest and transparent, we are often most careless with the words we speak to people closest to us. In contrast, so much more thought, time, and effort are often spent on preparing what is said to a room full of strangers who we are trying to impress.

THE POWER OF WORDS

I dream of taking back many words I have said over the past years. Words that have been overheard by others who I was not speaking to directly. Sometimes I feel like Mother telling me her story when I was eleven—I just want to stand up and scream—"Do you not understand what you are doing and WHO you are influencing with your everyday spoken words?" May we never forget that "the human tongue is a beast that few people can master. It strains constantly to break out of its cage, and if it is not tamed, it will run wild and cause harmful hurt and grief."[41]

I have thought a lot about the power of our words. Our words can either bring life or bring death; can either build up or tear down. We have *the power to give life to our thoughts* through the words we speak—we can speak a message into existence—that is the power of our words.

If we could really grasp the truth of these words every one of us could MAKE A NEW LIFECHANGING MESSAGE INSTEAD OF REPRODUCING OUR MESS. Think about it...*we could exchange our mess for a lifegiving message,* literally.

I have had numerous conversations with my grandchildren about what they think about *the power of words* and how they affect people. I think they have a pretty good grasp about why our words matter and how important it is that we use our words wisely.

When asked about the power of our words, my grandson Trevor replied with a line from a movie, "The problem is not the problem; the problem is your attitude behind the problem."[42] Then he said to me inquisitively, "Do you know who said that?" I said, "No. I have no idea." He quickly responded in his best pirate voice, "Captain Jack Sparrow!" I must tell you, that brought a smile to my face; because, now that I have watched the movie all the way through—I love *Pirates of the Caribbean*! However, when I asked Trevor how this related to "the power of words" he quickly replied, "Your attitude affects your words." I think this grandson gets it—and I could not have loved his response more.

The other grandchildren chimed in with amazing responses. Ever the realist, my granddaughter, Brooke, shared a quote from John F. Kennedy, "If we are strong, our strength will speak for itself. If we are weak, words will not be able to help us."

My kindhearted Ciera said, "Be sure to taste your words before spitting them out!"[43]

And Alli, who is deeply intuitive, said, "Do not mix bad words with your bad mood. You will have many opportunities to change your mood, but you will never have the chance to replace the words you spoke."

Brittany, who is often reserved quietly said, "Words hurt you more than anything because they last, and sometimes forever."

My grandson Keaton spoke up and said, "What screws us up most in life is the picture in our head of how we think things are supposed to be. This can interfere with good communication and cause us to choose words that may be inappropriate in the moment."

And grandson Grayson most recently said, "Words can break someone into a million pieces, but they can also put them back together again. I hope we use our words for good, because the only words you will regret more than the ones left unsaid, are the ones used to intentionally hurt someone." Another statement of truth.

BAD TEMPER AND A BAG OF NAILS

Because, I truly believe that the words we speak have more power than we can possibly imagine, I want to share with you one last story that poignantly illustrates the importance of our words. I hope the story will stay with you forever the way my mother's story has stayed with me since the day I heard her tell it to me when I was eleven years old. I do not know the author of this story, but it bears repeating.

There once was a little boy who had a bad temper. His father gave him a bag of nails and told him that every time he lost his temper, instead of uttering hurtful words, he must hammer a nail into the fence. The first day the boy had driven 37 nails into the fence. Over the next few weeks, as he learned to control his anger, the number of nails hammered daily gradually dwindled down. He discovered it was easier to hold his temper than to drive those nails into the fence.

Finally, the day came when the boy did not lose his temper at all. He told his father about it and the father suggested that the boy now pull out one nail for each day he was able to hold his temper. The days passed and the young boy was finally able to tell his father that all the nails were gone.

The father took his son by the hand and led him to the fence. He said, "You have done well, my son, but look at the holes in the fence. The fence will never be the same. When you say things in anger, they leave a scar just like this one. You can put a knife in a man and draw it out. It won't matter how many times you say, "I'm sorry," the wound is still there.

The little boy then understood how powerful his words were. He looked up at his father and said, "I hope you can forgive me father for the holes I put in you." "Of course, I can," said the father.

Mercifully and lovingly, this young man's father forgave him. And yes, we must forgive when someone wounds us with the words they speak, because Jesus' Father tells us that *forgiveness is a choice-based decision, not emotions-based* decision; this kind of forgiveness is a *personal release*, not an inauthentic condoning. This is true, even though wounds may be very deep, and scars can last a lifetime—all from the words we utter. *Unforgiveness is a malignant cancer—early detection and decisive removal leads to the cure.*

KINDNESS AND CHARACTER OVERFLOWING

"Cat's In The Cradle" is replaying in the background of my mind as I write. And, it is not only *father* I am envisioning, I am also envisioning *mother* and *role models* of all types, shapes, sizes, and ages. Incidents at school lead to detention and parent-teacher conferences. But what good does that do when a child knows those words were heard first at home from a parent's mouth, or on a practice field from a coach's mouth, or overheard outside the faculty lunchroom door? When asked "Why are you speaking this way?" must a child also *difunctionally* lie or must the child *honestly* answer with what he or she knows the answer to be. *What are we doing to our children?* who are like super sponges taking in everything they hear and see their parents, guardians, and role models do? Who else are they going to learn from at such early ages?

KINDNESS overflowing is what children, yours, mine, and ours deserve. *Kindness Overflowing.* CHARACTER *without excuses* OVERFLOWING is what children, yours, mine, and ours deserve.

If we would but realize that it is very simple to *speak* words of kindness and to *offer* genuine sincere compliments and encouragement for the building up of our families, we would then discover that the family compass always points to home. Above everything else, home should be the place where love and kindness are the first and last thing, we feel every morning and every evening and all the times in between *with the people we are the closest to* in this crazy, mixed up, confusing world.

Our home is where we *learn or do not learn* kindness and character. It is where our *perception of normal* becomes distorted or clear. T.S. Elliott defines hell as loneliness; many days family members come home to feel loneliness instead of kindness and love. It is very simple to speak words of kindness, compliment, encourage, and build up every day.

Lelia Schott explains "Perhaps if tearful little boys were comforted kindly instead of shamed, there would not be so many angry men struggling to express and empathize with their emotions." Even unintentional inattention is destructive.

Many of us were taught to "Treat people *the way you expect* to be treated" but far too many of us expect to be treated badly. Healthy expectation is often a struggle, especially when we have no idea of what we *could, should, or would* even *like* to expect. So, we must learn *how* to expect better *of* and *for* ourselves.

You may encounter badly behaved, taught, or trained people in various ways throughout the day at school, work, in the grocery store, or on the highways. They may not treat you or speak to you with kindness. But we have the choice not to replicate their treatment.

This is not rocket science. This is not difficult. This is a simple significant choice to make.

Choose to become the *make a difference person* you were created to be!

Put your past negative experiences of mistreatment aside. When you look into the eyes of the people who trust, look up to, and love you where you are NOW.

Thoughts lead to attitudes and emotions—choose them wisely. There is a reason scripture encourages us to "take *every* thought captive in the obedience to Christ."[44] *Destructive* thoughts have no place in our lives so they must be taken to Him for *incarceration. Constructive* thoughts must be given the place they deserve because He uses them for our *instruction.* Choose thoughts like you are choosing from a menu—when you say Yes to one, you are saying No to the rest.

Choose the Life you want for yourself and for those you love, then take steps with them to have it!

Thoughts lead to attitudes and emotions—these lead to words and agreements when choosing what is best for all concerned. Selfish words lead to disagreement, are we surprised? Agreements with "what is wise and worth working for" leads to action and results that produce *a life worth living!*

Words are the ingredients of Your Story, *common or Uncommon*—it is yours to decide!

The time is here, the time is now! It is time for you to begin to *make a new-lifechanging-message out of an old-reproducing-mess!*

The Fight FOR FAMILY is a fight for a better future, a fight for worthwhile goals, a fight that will not give up, a fight for what can only be done empowered by God in our generation and the next. Winning TOGETHER IS AN UNCOMMON STORY worth telling for generations to come! What will be said about your part in your family's story for years to come? Consider the best story and the best ending. Then, let God give you His wisdom, power, and love to LIVE IT!

About the Author

Francie Willis began her professional career with the Wendy Ward Charm School coaching over 6,000 young women in a short span of six years. Her experience led her to the staff of Miss Teenage America as event choreographer and to the development of a nationwide Business Etiquette Program for Women. Traveling across the nation, she made presentations to Fortune 500 companies, and consulted with management staff of corporations in the USA. Including IBM, 3M, Coca Cola, General Electric, Xerox, Chevron, CBS, Sara Lee, & Eastman Kodak.

As a visionary entrepreneur, Francie Willis took a pioneering step when she opened Urban Retreat, a luxury day spa and salon in the heart of River Oaks, Houston, Texas. Within four years after opening her industry transforming business, *Modern Salon* and *Spa*, the two leading industry magazines, named Urban Retreat the 1993 Spa of the Year. As Co-Founder and CEO of Urban Retreat, her success has been recognized by *Allure, Better Homes & Gardens, Elle, Redbook, Vogue, Harper's Bazaar, Town and Country, Women's World, Seventeen, People* and *Day Spa Magazine*.

With her reputation well established, Willis opened Urban Retreat West Day Spa and The Urban Retreat Skin Care Center and

Medi Spa. Utilizing the knowledge gained from her skin care research and experience, she gained notoriety in the cosmetics industry creating Franché® Mineral Cosmetics (the first mineral-based makeup with freeze-dried vitamins and sun protection factor (SPF) 20 and Franché® Chirally Correct Skin Care. Franché® launched at the celebrated Henri Bendel department store in New York. The development of her skin care line included products for women, men, and children.

Francie Willis' name graced the *Houston Business Journal* "Top 50 Women Business Owners" list for ten consecutive years. She has had a leading philanthropic and community service presence in Houston for the past 25 years. She has served on the boards of three educational institutions, including the University of Houston. Her leadership as chairperson of 16 galas made possible the raising of more than ten million dollars for Houston charities, including the Chiquapin Preparatory School, The Monarch School, the Moore School of Music, the University of Houston, the Houston Grand Opera, and the Houston Gulf Coast Chapter of Sickle Cell.

Willis has been the recipient of numerous awards, including the *Grandmother of the Year* and *Inspiring Business Woman of the Year* by The Inspire Women's Organization, the Houston *Treasure Award* by the Social Book of Texas, *Business Entrepreneur* and *Business Woman of the Year* by the Texas Women's Chamber of Commerce, *Community Hero Award* by the Houston Fire Museum, *Distinguished Service Award* by the University of Houston HAO, *"Windows of Opportunity" Business & Entrepreneur Honoree* by Benefiting Inner City Kids with Scholarships, *Lifetime Volunteer* by the Citizens for Animal Protection (CAP), *Top 25 Houston Leaders and Legends,* and *Volunteer of the Year* by The National Association of Fund-Raising Executives, *Humanitarian of The Year* by the Cleveland Amory

National Association, and *Business Woman of the Year* by the national organization A Tribute to Business Women.

Notes

[1] Eph. 3:20 (paraphrase)

[2] Rev. 21:15 KJV

[3] Mark Batterson; In a Pit with a Lion on A Snowy Day, (Colorado Springs, CO: Multnomah,2016),32

[4] Apollo 13. Screenplay by William Broyles Jr and Al Reinert. Dir. Ron Howard. Special Edition DVD. Universal Pictures, 1995

[5] Janet Geringer Woititz, Adult Children of Alcoholics, (Deerfield Beach, FL: Health Communications, Inc, 1983)

[6] John 10:10 ESV

[7] Jer. 29:11 NLT

[8] Rom. 5:8; KNT

[9] I Sam. 17:47 NABRE

[10] Phil. 4:13 BSB

[11] Rom. 3:23 CEV

[12] John 15:11 AMP

[13] Heb. 12:2 CSB

[14] Heb. 11:1 HCSB

[15] Ibid.

[16] Matt. 19:26 NKJV

[17] John 2: 5, 7 ESV

[18] N.T. Wright, John For Everyone, Part 2, (London, England and Louisville, KY: Society for Promoting Christian Knowledge, and Westminster John Knox Press, 2004),49

[19] John 14:18 NKJV

[20] Ibid. CSB

[21] Boban Docevski, The Vintage News, January 5, 2018

[22] Ps. 139:13-18 CJB

[23] I Cor. 12:4-6, 11 NLT

[24] Gal. 6:4 NIV

[25] Gen. 3 :1 CSB

[26] Gen. 15 :5 NLT (paraphrase mine)

[27] 1 Cor. 12: 17 CJB

[28] Howe, Mrs. Dr. S. G. [Julia Ward]. Battle Hymn of The Republic. Boston, MA: Oliver Ditson & Co., 1862.

[29] Luke 2:49 KJB

[30] I Cor. 13:5 KNT
[31] I Cor. 13:11 TPT
[32] Ps. 139:16-17 TPT
[33] Ez. 36:26-28 MSG
[34] Billy Graham Daily Devotions: The Power of Words. September 17. https://billygraham.org/devotion/the-power-of-words/ (accessed April 18, 2019)
[35] Piper, John and Taylor, Justin. The Power of Words and The Wonder of God. DesiringGod.org. https://www.desiringgod.org/books/the-power-of-words-and-the-wonder-of-god (accessed April 15, 2019).
[36] Mark 12 :31 NIV (paraphrase mine)
[37] Prov. 23 :7 AKJV
[38] Eph. 4:29 NIV
[39] Ibid.
[40] Col. 4:6 NIV
[41] https://www.goodreads.com/work/quotes/1297604-the-48-laws-of-power?page=3; Robert Green: The 48 Laws of Power
[42] Pirates of The Caribbean: The Curse of The Black Pearl. Screenplay by Ted Elliot and Terry Rossio. Dir. Jerry Bruckheimer. Walt Disney Pictures, July 9, 2003
[43] Ice, Auliq. Quotable Quotes. https://www.goodreads.com/quotes/7079509-be-sure-to-taste-your-words-before-you-spit-them (accessed April 15, 2019)
[44] 2 Cor. 10:5 NABRE

Francie Willis' Previous Published Works

Marchione, Francie, *"Sugar & Spice"*, (Etiquette and Charm for the 6-8-year-old Princess), Houston, Texas/ Madison Press, 1978.

Marchione, Francie, *"Pre-Teen Answers"*, (Etiquette, Charm and Natural Beauty for the Pre-Teen), Houston, Texas/Madison Press, 1978.

Marchione, Francie, *"A Guide to Teen Age Beauty"*, Houston, Texas/ Madison Press, 1978.

Willis, Francie, *"Bonna Comes To America"*, Houston, Texas/Francie Willis Publishing Co. Francie Willis Books for Young Readers, 1993.

Made in the USA
San Bernardino, CA
18 January 2020